AUTOBIOGRAPHY,

POEMS AND SONGS

OF

ELLEN JOHNSTON,

THE 'FACTORY GIRL.'

GLASGOW:
WILLIAM LOVE, 40 ST ENOCH SQUARE,
MDCCCLXVII.

This scarce antiquarian book is included in our special *Legacy Reprint Series*. In the interest of creating a more extensive selection of rare historical book reprints, we have chosen to reproduce this title even though it may possibly have occasional imperfections such as missing and blurred pages, missing text, poor pictures, markings, dark backgrounds and other reproduction issues beyond our control. Because this work is culturally important, we have made it available as a part of our commitment to protecting, preserving and promoting the world's literature.

Dedicated

TO ALL MEN AND WOMEN OF EVERY CLASS,

SECT, AND PARTY,

WHO BY THEIR SKILL, LABOUR, 'SCIENCE,

ART, LITERATURE, AND POETRY,

PROMOTE THE

MORAL AND SOCIAL ELEVATION OF HUMANITY,

BY THEIR OBEDIENT SERVANT,

ELLEN JOHNSTON,

THE FACTORY GIRL.

INDEX.

POEMS.

Title	Page
Address to Napiers' Dockyard,	9
My Mother,	12
A Brother Poet,	13
Lines on the Death of a Beloved Child,	13
The Maniac of the Green Wood,	15
Kennedy's Dear Mill,	19
Childhood's Flowers: The Gowan and the Buttercup,	21
The Morning: A Recitation,	23
The Factory Exile,	25
The Absent Husband,	27
Welcome, Garibaldi!	28
Mourning for Garibaldi,	29
The Parting,	30
The 'Workman' for Ever,	32
The Lost Lover,	33
The Suicide,	34
Love Outwitted,	36
The Happy Man,	38
The Rifleman's Melody,	40
Love and War,	42
A Mother's Love,	44
To my Aunt Phemie,	45
An Appeal,	47
Lovely Johnie White,	48
Farewell,	50
Lines to a Lovely Youth,	51
Lines to Mr and Mrs B.,	52
The Broken Heart: A Tale,	54
On the Loss of the Dalhousie,	57
The Summer's Away,	58
The Drunkard's Wife,	59
Address to the High Church of Glasgow on the Rash Judgment of Man,	61
Lines to a Young Gentleman of Surpassing Beauty,	62
The Marriage Morning,	63
Lines on Miss Margaret Dorward sending her Carte de Visite and Bouquet of Flowers to the Authoress,	65
Lines Dedicated to James Kennedy, Esq., of Bedford Street Weaving Factory, Belfast,	66
The Husband's Lament,	68
The Exile of Poland,	69
Epitaph,	70
The Lay of a Scottish Girl,	71
The Ruined Heiress,	73
The Wrongs of Mary Queen of Scots,	74
The Forsaken Maiden,	76
The Baxter Statue,	77

INDEX.

	PAGE
The Working Man,	79
My Cousin Bill,	80
Perjury's Victim,	81
Lines on behalf of the Boatbuilders and Boilermakers of Great Britain and Ireland,	83
Lines to Mr James Dorward, Power-Loom Foreman, Chapelshade Works, Dundee,	86
Your Wee Neebour Nell,	88
Lines to a Sick Friend,	89
The Drygate Brae; or, Wee Mary's First Love,	90
Address to Kelvin Water,	91
The Factory Girl's Farewell,	93
The Lost Purse,	96
Address to the Factory of Messrs J. & W. L. Scott & Co., John Street, Bridgeton,	97
The Last Sark,	100
Lines Dedicated to Mr James Dorward,	101
The Opening of the Baxter Park,	102
Lines in Memory of Mary Watson Parker,	104
Galbraith's Trip,	106
Tennants' Excursion,	109
Lines to R. H. P., Parkhead,	113
Lines to G. D. Russell,	115
Lines to G. D. Russell, late of St. Ninian's, Stirling,	116
Lines to R. H. P., Parkhead,	118
The Factory Girl's Address to her Muse,	119
Lines to Mr Colin Steel, from his old Schoolmate and Companion, 'The Factory Girl,'	121
The Shoemaker's Wife,	123
The British Lion,	124
Auld Dunville,	125
O Come awa', Jamie,	127
Nelly's Lament for the Pirnhouse Cat,	128
A Satire on a Pretended Friend,	130
Mrs Cooper,	132
Wee Poet Nell,	133
The Peacock,	134
The Fourpence-piece,	135
Lines to Mr Alex. Campbell,	136
Lines to the Memory of a Beloved Wife,	138
Address to my Brother Bards,	139
Address to Nature on its Cruelty,	141
The Trip o' Blochairn,	143

POETIC ADDRESSES & RESPONSES.

A Farewell Address, written before leaving for Queensland,	145
Lines Respectfully Dedicated by various Contributors, 146 to 154 161, 167, 171, 175, 176,	179
The Maid o' Dundee,	152
Lines to Mr B. Smith, Glasgow,	155
Lines by Edith to the Factory Girl,	156
The Factory Girl's Reply to 'Lines by Edith,'.	157
Edith's Reply to the Factory Girl,	159
The Factory Girl's Reply to Edith,	163

INDEX.

	PAGE
The Factory Girl's Reply to David Morrison, Caldervale, Airdrie,	165
Lines to the Factory Girl, by a Glasgow Lassie,	168
The Factory Girl's Reply to 'A Glasgow Lassie,'	169
Lines to Mr G. D. Russell, Queensland, accompanied with a Carte de Visite of 'The Factory Girl,'	172
To Scotia's Hard-Toiling Girl,	177
To the Poet,	180
Lines to Edith, with G. D. Russell's and the Factory Girl's Cartes,	182
Lines by Edith, on Receiving the Cartes of Mr Russell and the Factory Girl,	185
Lines to Mr Daniel Syme, Lanark,	187
Lines to Ellen, the Factory Girl,	189
Lines to Isabel from the Factory Girl,	190
Lines to Mr David Morrison, Caldervale,	193

SONGS.

The Lad of Burnbank Mill,	196
Broken Vows,	197
Bogle and I,	197
We've Parted,	199
My Childhood's Hours,	200
The Young Man's Darling,	201
A Voice from the Mountains,	202
O! Scotland, My Country,	203
A Song of War,	205
My Maggie,	207
The Miller Lad,	207
The Nicht I Married Tom,	208
The Thistle Hall,	209
Lord Raglan's Address to the Allied Armies,	211
The Lass o' the Glen,	213
Francis Best,	214
The Lasses o' Dundee,	215
My Bonnie Donald Kay,	216
Kennedy's Factory for Ever,	217
Lintfield, the Boast of Green Erin,	219
The Weekly News in the Morning,	221
Rhyming Nelly (First Version),	222
Do. (Second Version),	223
Wanted, A Man,	224
Song,	226

APPENDIX.

The Maid of Dundee to her Slumbering Muse,	227
Welcome and Appeal for the Maid of Dundee,	230

TESTIMONIAL.

FROM THE REV. GEORGE GILFILLAN.

DUNDEE, 21st *July*, 1866.

ELLEN JOHNSTON, the 'Factory Girl,' has asked me to look over her verses. This I have done with very considerable interest and pleasure. She labours, of course, under great disadvantage, but subtracting all the signs of imperfect education, her rhymes are highly creditable to her heart and head too—are written always with fluency and often with sweetness, and, I see, have attracted the notice and the warm praise of many of her own class. I hope she will be encouraged by this to cultivate her mind, to read to correct the faults in her style—arising from her limited opportunities—and so doing, she cannot fail to secure still increased respect and warmer patronage.

GEORGE GILFILLAN.

List of Subscribers.

The following, among others, have subscribed for the Autobiography, Poems, and Songs of Ellen Johnston, the Factory Girl :—

DUKE OF BUCCLEUCH, ... 4 Copies.
EARL OF ENNISKILLEN.
Major-General Sir VINCENT EYRE, R.A., K.C.S.I., C.B.
SIR JOHN BOWRING.
Colonel SYKES, M.P., London.
DAVID JOBSON, Jun., Esq., 40 Castle Street.
O. G. MILLER, Esq., Meadowside.
T. K. KINMOND, Esq.
A. MATHIESON, Esq., Union Street.
J. P. SMITH, Esq., C.E., Glasgow.
Mrs HARE, 41 Brook Street, Grosvenor Square, London.
JOHN RIDLEY, Esq., 19 Belsize Park, London.
WALTER WELDON, Esq., Park Villa, West Hill, Highgate, London.
M. CUNIGE, Esq., 32 Great St Helen's, London. . . 2 Copies.
JOS. BOSWORTH, D.D., F.R.S., F.S.A., &c., Professor of Anglo-Saxon, Oxford.
J. H. BELL, Dundee.
BISHOP OF BRECHIN.
Colonel KINLOCH, Logie, Kirriemuir.
T. L. TAKEDA, Esq., 19 Marischal Street, Aberdeen.
Professor M'DONALD, St Andrews.
Mrs E. PARKER, The Cliff, Dundee.
JOS. GARSIDE, Esq., Selby, Yorkshire.
THOS. J. MOORE, Kennessee Green, Maghull, Liverpool.
G. J. BROWN, M.D., 31 Bon-Accord Terrace, Aberdeen.
J. JACK, Esq., Belhelvie, Aberdeenshire.
JAMES ABERNETHY, Esq., Ferry Hill, Aberdeen.
WM. SMITH, Esq., 18 Salisbury Street, Strand, London.
B. G. WOOD, Esq., F.G.S., Richmond, Yorkshire.
JAMES M. SMITH, F.R.S., LL.D., 8 Castle Street, Dundee.

W. J. Macqueen Rankine, Esq., C.E., LL.D.
John Ritchie, Esq., Dundee.
Henry Blyth, Esq., Dundee.
John Sharp, Esq., Dundee.
William Harvey, Carnowdie, Dundee.
George Ireland, jun., 15 Wellington Street.
R. H. Wybrants, Esq., 1 Laurel Bank.
George Owen, Esq., 2 Union Terrace.
Ellen Johnston, Dundee, for Subscribers, . . 20 copies.
James Dorward and Peter Cant, Dundee, for themselves and other subscribers, ... 22 do
Daniel Sym, for self and others, ... 6 do.
Peter M'Call, Ayr, for self and others, . . . 5 do.
D. Pettigrew, New Road, Parkhead, for self and others, ... 4 do.
Alex. Campbell, ... 8 do.
David Morrison, Caldervale, for self and others, . 14 do.
Cecilia Bigham, Glasgow, for self and others, . . 3 do.
James Cranston, Glasgow,
William Carswell, Chirmorrie, by Girvan.
R. H. P., Parkhead.
Alexander Gartshore.
Mrs Douglas, Galashiels.
William Paterson.
Mrs Menzies.
Miss Grant.
Miss Margaret Shanks.
Robert Harvey, Glasgow.
Mrs Melville, do.
John Annan.
William Crawford.
John Waggstaff, Ayr.
John Arris, Donaldson Lodge, near Coldstream.

N.B—In addition to the preceding list there are a number of other Subscribers whose names have not reached the printers in time for this Edition.

AUTOBIOGRAPHY

OF

ELLEN JOHNSTON,

'THE FACTORY GIRL.'

GENTLE READER,—On the suggestion of a friend, and the expressed wishes of some subscribers, I now submit the following brief sketch of my eventful life as an introduction to this long expected and patiently waited for volume of my Poems and Songs.

Like every other autobiographer, I can only relate the events connected with my parentage and infancy from the communicated evidence of witnesses of those events, but upon whose veracity I have full reliance.

I beg also to remind my readers that whatever my actions may have been, whether good, bad, or indifferent, that they were the results of instincts derived from the Creator, through the medium of my parents, and the character formed for me by the unavoidable influence of the TIME and COUNTRY of my BIRTH, and also by the varied conditions of life impressing themselves on my highly susceptible and sympathetic natures—physical, intellectual, and moral.

According to the evidence referred to, my father was James Johnston, second eldest son of James Johnston, canvas-weaver, Lochee, Dundee, where he learned the trade of a stone-mason. After which he removed to Glasgow, where he became acquainted with my mother, Mary Bilsland, second daughter of James Bilsland, residing in Muslin Street, and then well known as the Bridgeton Dyer.

I do not remember hearing my father's age, but my mother at the time of her marriage was only eighteen years old. I was the first and only child of their union, and was born in the Muir Wynd, Hamilton, in 183—, my father at the time being employed as a mason extending the northern wing of the Duke of Hamilton's Palace.

When the Duke was informed that my father was a poet, he familiarly used to call him Lord Byron, and, as I have been told, his Grace also used to take special notice of me when an infant in my mother's arms, as she almost daily walked around his domain.

When I was about seven months old my father's contract at Hamilton Palace was finished, and being of an active disposition, somewhat ambitious, proud, and independent, with some literary and scientific attainments, with a strong desire to become a teacher and publish a volume of his poetical works, he resolved to emigrate, engaged a passage to America for my mother and himself, and got all things ready for the voyage.

But when all the relatives and friends had assembled at the Broomielaw to give the farewell kiss and shake of the hand before going on board, my mother determined not to proceed, pressed me

THE FACTORY GIRL.

fondly to her bosom, exclaiming—'I cannot, will not go, my child would die on the way;' and taking an affectionate farewell with my father, he proceeded on the voyage, and my mother fled from the scene and returned to her father's house, where she remained for some years, and supported herself by dressmaking and millinery.

Having given the evidence of others in respect to my parentage and infancy, let me now, gentle reader, state some of my own childhood's recollections, experience, and reflections thereon.

In my childhood, Bridgeton now incorporated with the city of Glasgow, abounded with green fields and lovely gardens, which have since then been covered over with piles of buildings and tall chimneys. The ground on which the factory of Messrs Scott & Inglis stands was then a lovely garden, where I spent many, many happy hours with 'Black Bess,' my doll, and 'Dainty Davie,' my dog, with whom I climbed many a knowe and forded many a stream, till one day he left my side to follow a band of music, and we never met again; but for whose loss I deeply mourned, and for three successive nights wept myself asleep, for 'Dainty Davie' was the pride of my heart, for I could not live without something to love, and I loved before I knew the name of the nature or feeling which swelled my bosom.

Perhaps there are few who can take a retrospective view of their past lives, and through their mind's eye gaze on so many strange and mysterious incidents. Yes, gentle reader, I have suffered trials and wrongs that have but rarely fallen to the lot of woman. Mine were not the common trials of every day life, but like those strange romantic ordeals attributed to the imaginary heroines of 'Inglewood Forest.'

Like the Wandering Jew, I have mingled with the gay on the shores of France—I have feasted in the merry halls of England—I have danced on the shamrock soil of Erin's green isle—

and I have sung the songs of the brave and the free in the woods and glens of dear old Scotland.

I have waited and watched the sun-set hour to meet my lover, and then with him wander by the banks of sweet winding Clutha, when my muse has often been inspired when viewing the proud waving thistle bending to the breeze, or when the calm twilight hour was casting a halo of glory around the enchanting scene; yet in all these wanderings I never enjoyed true happiness.

Like Rassellas, there was a dark history engraven on the tablet of my heart. Yes, dear reader, a dark shadow, as a pall, enshrouded my soul, shutting out life's gay sunshine from my bosom—a shadow which has haunted me like a vampire, but at least for the present must remain the mystery of my life.

Dear reader, I have wandered far away from my childhood's years. Yes, years that passed like a dream, unclouded and clear. Oh that I could recall them; but, alas! they are gone for ever. Still they linger in memory fresh and green as if they were yesterday. I can look back and see the opening chapters of my life—I can see the forms and faces, and hear their voices ringing in my ears—one sweet voice above the rest echoes like a seraph's song; but I dare not linger longer at present with those joyous hours and beloved forms that were then my guardian angels.

In the course of time my mother received some information of my father's death in America, and again married a power-loom tenter when I was about eight years of age, till which time I may truly say that the only heartfelt sorrow I experienced was the loss of 'Dainty Davie;' but, alas! shortly after my mother's second marriage I was dragged, against my own will and the earnest pleadings and remonstrance of my maternal grandfather, from his then happy home to my stepfather's abode, next land to the Cross Keys Tavern, London Road.

THE FACTORY GIRL.

HOW I BECAME THE FACTORY GIRL.

About two months after my mother's marriage my stepfather having got work in a factory in Bishop Street, Anderston, they removed to North Street, where I spent the two last years of young life's sweet liberty—as it was during that time I found my way to Kelvin Grove, and there spent many happy hours in innocent mirth and glee—but 'time changes a' things.' My stepfather could not bear to see me longer basking in the sunshine of freedom, and therefore took me into the factory where he worked to learn power-loom weaving when about eleven years of age, from which time I became a factory girl; but no language can paint the suffering which I afterwards endured from my tormentor.

Before I was thirteen years of age I had read many of Sir Walter Scott's novels, and fancied I was a heroine of the modern style. I was a self-taught scholar, gifted with a considerable amount of natural knowledge for one of my years, for I had only been nine months at school when I could read the English language and Scottish dialect with almost any classic scholar; I had also read 'Wilson's Tales of the Border;' so that by reading so many love adventures my brain was fired with wild imaginations, and therefore resolved to bear with my own fate, and in the end gain a great victory.

I had also heard many say that I ought to have been an actress, as I had a flow of poetic language and a powerful voice, which was enough to inspire my young soul to follow the profession. In fact, I am one of those beings formed by nature for romance and mystery, and as such had many characters to imitate in the course of a day. In the residence of my stepfather I was a weeping willow, in the factory I was pensive and thoughtful, dreaming of the far off future when I would be hailed as a 'great star.' Then, when mixing with a merry company no one could be more cheerful, for I had learned to conceal my own cares and sorrows, knowing well that 'the mirth maker hath no sympathy with the grief weeper.'

By this time my mother had removed from Anderston to a shop in Tradeston, and my stepfather and myself worked in West Street Factory. When one morning early, in the month of June, I absconded from their house as the fox flies from the hunters' hounds, to the Paisley Canal, into which I was about submerging myself to end my sufferings and sorrow, when I thought I heard like the voice of him I had fixed my girlish love upon. I started and paused for a few moments, and the love of young life again prevailed over that of self-destruction, and I fled from the scene as the half-past five morning factory bells were ringing, towards the house of a poor woman in Rose Street, Hutchesontown, where, after giving her my beautiful earrings to pawn, I was made welcome, and on Monday morning following got work in Brown & M'Nee's factory, Commercial Road. I did not, however, remain long in my new lodgings, for on the Tuesday evening, while threading my way among the crowd at the shows, near the foot of Saltmarket, and busy dreaming of the time when I would be an actress, I was laid hold of by my mother's eldest brother, who, after questioning me as to where I had been, and what I was doing, without receiving any satisfaction to his interrogations, compelled me to go with him to my mother, who first questioned me as to the cause of absconding, and then beat me till I felt as if my brain were on fire; but still I kept the secret in my own bosom. But had I only foreseen the wretched misery I was heaping upon my own head—had I heard the dreadful constructions the world was putting on my movements—had I seen the shroud of shame and sorrow I was weaving around myself, I should then have disclosed the mystery of my life, but I remained silent and kept my mother and friends in ignorance of the cause which first disturbed my peace and made me run away from her house for safety and protection.

However, I consented to stay again with my mother for a time, and resolved to avoid my tormentor as much as possible.

Weeks and months thus passed away, but, alas! the sun never shed the golden dawn of peaceful morn again around my mother's hearth. Apart from my home sorrows I had other trials to encounter. Courted for my conversation and company by the most intelligent of the factory workers, who talked to me about poets and poetry, which the girls around me did not understand, consequently they wondered, became jealous, and told falsehoods of me. Yet I never fell out with them although I was a living martyr, and suffered all their insults. In fact, life had no charm for me but one, and that was my heart's first love. If a sunshine of pleasure ever fell upon me, it was in his company only for a few short moments, for nothing could efface from my memory the deep grief that pressed me to the earth. I often smiled when my heart was weeping—the gilded mask of false merriment made me often appear happy in company when I was only playing the dissembler.

Dear reader, as this is neither the time nor place to give farther details of my young eventful life, I will now bring you to my sixteenth year, when I was in the bloom of fair young maidenhood. Permit me, however, to state that during the three previous years of my life, over a part of which I am drawing a veil, I had run away five times from my tormentor, and during one of those elopements spent about six weeks in Airdrie, wandering often by Carron or Calder's beautiful winding banks. Oh! could I then have seen the glorious gems that have sprung up for me on those banks, and heard the poetic strains that have since been sung in my praise, what a balm they would have been to my bleeding heart, as I wandered around the old Priestrig Pit and listened to its engine thundering the water up from its lowest depth. For days I have wandered the fields between Moodiesburn and Clifton Hill, wooing my sorry muse, then unknown to the world—except to a few, as a child of song—in silence looking forward to the day when the world would know my wrongs and prize my worth; and had it not been for the bright Star of Hope which lingered near me and encouraged me onward, beyond doubt I would have been a suicide. 'Tis, however, strange in all my weary wanderings that I have always met with kind-hearted friends, and there were two who befriended me when I was a homeless wanderer in Airdrie. Fifteen years have passed since I saw their tears roll down the youthful cheeks and heard the heavy sigh that exploded from their sympathising hearts. But the best of friends must part, and I parted with them, perhaps never to meet again in this lovely world of sunshine and sorrow.

Dear reader, should your curiosity have been awakened to ask in what form fate had then so hardly dealt with the hapless 'Factory Girl,' this is my answer:—I was falsely accused by those who knew me as a fallen woman, while I was as innocent of the charge as the unborn babe. Oh! how hard to be blamed when the heart is spotless and the conscience clear. For years I submitted to this wrong, resolving to hold my false detractors at defiance.

While struggling under those misrepresentations, my first love also deserted me, but another soon after offered me his heart—without the form of legal protection—and in a thoughtless moment I accepted him as my friend and protector, but, to use the words of a departed poet—

> 'When lovely woman stoops to folly,
> And finds too late that men betray,
> What can sooth her melancholy,
> What can wash her guilt away?

THE FACTORY GIRL.

> The only art her guilt to cover,
> To hide her shame from every eye,
> To wring repentance from her lover,
> And sting his bosom, is to die.'

I did not, however, feel inclined to die when I could no longer conceal what the world falsely calls a woman's shame. No, on the other hand, I never loved life more dearly and longed for the hour when I would have something to love me—and my wish was realised by becoming the mother of a lovely daughter on the 14th of September, 1852.

No doubt, every feeling mother thinks her own child lovely, but mine was surpassing so, and I felt as if I could begin all my past sorrows again if Heaven would only spare me my lovely babe to cheer my bleeding heart, for I never felt bound to earth till then; and as year succeeded year, 'My Mary Achin' grew like the wild daisy—fresh and fair—on the mountain side.

As my circumstances in life changed, I placed my daughter under my mother's care when duty called me forth to turn the poetic gift that nature had given me to a useful and profitable account, for which purpose I commenced with vigorous zeal to write my poetical pieces, and sent them to the weekly newspapers for insertion, until I became extensively known and popular. As an instance, in 1854 the Glasgow Examiner published a song of mine, entitled 'Lord Raglan's Address to the Allied Armies,' which made my name popular throughout Great Britain and Ireland; but as my fame spread my health began to fail, so that I could not work any longer in a factory.

My stepfather was unable longer to work, and my mother was also rendered a suffering object; my child was then but an infant under three years of age, and I, who had been the only support of the family, was informed by my medical adviser that, unless I took a change of air, I would not live three months.

Under these circumstances, what was to be done? I did not then want to die, although I had wished to do so a thousand times before, to relieve me from unmerited slander and oppression.

Many sleepless nights did I pass, thinking what to try to bring relief to the afflicted household—although I did not consider myself in duty bound to struggle against the stern realities of nature, and sacrifice my own young life for those whose sympathies for me had been long seared and withered. Yet I could not, unmoved, look on the pale face of poverty, for their means were entirely exhausted, without hope to lean upon. Neither could I longer continue in the factory without certain death to myself, and I had never learned anything else.

Under those conflicting conditions and feelings, one night as I lay in bed, almost in despair, I prayed fervently that some idea how to act would be revealed to me, when suddenly I remembered that I had a piece of poetry entitled 'An Address to Napier's Dockyard, Lancefield, Finnieston,' which a young man had written for me in imitation of copperplate engraving, and that piece I addressed to Robert Napier, Esq., Shandon, Gareloch-head, who was then in Paris, where it was forwarded to him. Having written to my employer for my character, which was satisfactory, Mr Napier sent me a note to call at a certain office in Oswald Street, Glasgow, and draw as much money as would set me up in some small business, to see if my health would revive. According to the good old gentleman's instructions, I went as directed, and sought L.10, which was freely given to me; and I believe had I asked double the amount I would have readily received it.

THE FACTORY GIRL.

Dear reader, I need not tell you what a godsend those ten pounds were to my distressed family, and kept me out of the factory during five months; after which I resumed work in Messrs Galbraith's Mill, St Rollox, Glasgow, where I continued till July, 1857, when my health again sank; and for a change of air I went to Belfast, where I remained two years, during which time I became so notorious for my poetic exploits that the little boys and girls used to run after me to get a sight of 'the little Scotch girl' their fathers and mothers spoke so much about.

In 1859 I left Belfast and went to Manchester, where I worked three months, and then returned again to my native land, much improved in body and mind.

New scenes and systems made a great change in my natures. I became cheerful, and sought the society of mirthmakers, so that few would have taken me for the former moving monument of melancholy. I had again resumed work at Galbraith's factory, and all went on well. 'My bonnie Mary Auchinvole' was growing prettier every day and I was growing strong; peace and good-will reigned in our household, the past seemed forgiven and forgotten, and the 'Factory Girl' was a topic of the day for her poetical productions in the public press, but the shadow of death was hovering behind all this gladsome sunshine.

My mother had been an invalid for several years, and, to add to her sorrow, a letter had come from her supposed dead husband, my father, in America, after an absence of twenty years, inquiring for his wife and child; on learning their fate he became maddened with remorse, and, according to report, drank a death-draught from a cup in his own hand; and my mother, after becoming aware of the mystery of my life, closed her weary pilgrimage on earth on 25th May, 1861. Thus I was left without a friend, and disappointed of a future promised home and pleasure which I was not destined to enjoy, I therefore made up my mind to go to

AUTOBIOGRAPHY OF ELLEN JOHNSTON,

Dundee, where my father's sister resided, whose favourite I was when a child.

Dear reader, were I to give details of my trials, disappointments, joys, and sorrows, since I came to 'bonnie Dundee,' they would be, with a little embellishment, a romance of real life, sufficient to fill three ordinary volumes. Suffice here to say, that after myself and child had suffered neglect and destitution for some time, I got work in the Verdant Factory, where the cloth I wove was selected by my master as a sample for others to imitate, until, on the 5th of December, 1863, I was discharged by the foreman without any reason assigned or notice given, in accordance with the rules of the work. Smarting under this treatment, I summoned the foreman into Court for payment of a week's wages for not receiving notice, and I gained the case. But if I was envied by my sister sex in the Verdant Works for my talent before this affair happened, they hated me with a perfect hatred after I had struggled for and gained my rights. In fact, on account of that simple and just law-suit, I was persecuted beyond description—lies of the most vile and disgusting character were told upon me, till even my poor ignorant deluded sister sex went so far as to assault me on the streets, spit in my face, and even several times dragged the skirts from my dress. Anonymous letters were also sent to all the foremen and tenters not to employ me, so that for the period of four months after I wandered through Dundee a famished and persecuted factory exile.

From the foregoing statements some may think that I am rude, forward, and presumptuous, but permit me to say this much for myself, and those who know me best will confirm my statement, that I am naturally of a warm-hearted and affectionate disposition, always willing, to the extent of my power, to serve my fellow-creatures, and would rather endure an insult than retaliate on an enemy. All my wrongs have been suffered in silence and wept over in secret. It is the favour and fame of the poetic gift bestowed on me by nature's God that has brought on me the envy of the ignorant, for the enlightened classes of both sexes of factory workers love and admire me for my humble poetic effusions, so far as they have been placed before the public, but I merely mention this to clear away any doubt that may possibly arise in the mind of any of my readers.

In conclusion, I am glad to say that the persecution I was doomed to suffer in vindication not only of my own rights, but of the rights of such as might be similarly discharged, passed away, and peace and pleasure restored to my bosom again, by obtaining work at the Chapelshade Factory, at the east end of Dundee, where I have been working for the last three years and a-half to a true friend. I had not been long in my present situation when I fortunately became a reader of the 'Penny Post,' and shortly afterwards contributed some pieces to the 'Poet's Corner,' which seemed to cast a mystic spell over many of its readers whose numerous letters reached me from various districts, highly applauding my contributions, and offering me their sympathy, friendship, and love; while others, inspired by the muses, responded to me through the same popular medium some of whose productions will be found, along with my own in the present volume.

And now, gentle reader, let me conclude by offering my grateful thanks to the Rev. George Gilfillan for his testimony in respect to the merits of my poetic productions, to Mr Alex. Campbell, of the 'Penny Post,' for his services in promoting their publication, as well as to the subscribers who have so long patiently waited for this volume, which I hope may prove a means of social and intellectual enjoyment to many, and also help to relieve from the incessant toils of a factory life.

ELLEN JOHNSTON,
THE FACTORY GIRL.

OCTOBER, 1867.

POEMS.

An Address to Napiers' Dockyard,
LANCEFIELD, ANDERSTON.

HAIL! prince of public works—mechanic arts—
For men of genius and for noble hearts;
Honour and fame, peace, power, and merit,
Men well fill'd with philanthropic spirit.
   I cannot speak like scientific men
Whom literature gives colour to their pen,
Who clothe their genius in that golden robe
Wrought by learning, and not by nature's God.
Those gilded abstracts of high inspiration
Quoted out to gain man's admiration.
Give me origin—such I hold at bay
Who steal from authors of a bygone day;
Pampering pages with records unnumber'd
Robb'd from men who hath for centuries slumber'd.
   Nay, nay, dear Work, to thee I'll only speak!
Like what I am—a woman frail and weak.
My self-taught learning may have power to move,
For it is drawn from truth and heartfelt love,
Free from flattery and from language vain,
The sproutings of a love-sick woman's strain
Whose hopes are centered now within thy walls.
One of thy noble sons my heart enthrals!

No marvel then I love to breathe thy name,
It cheers my heart and fans a secret flame;
No marvel then I oft walk round thy dock,
Gazing intently on each secret spot,
Anxious to know when last my love stood there
That o'er it I might breathe a fervent prayer.
 Dear Work, you know not what a gorgeous sight
Thou art to me when wandering forth each night;
Inhaling the breeze of summer's flow'ry scene,
Musing on nature's lovely mantle green;
When all is still and silent as the grave,
When golden moonbeams kiss the silver wave
That rolleth gently o'er sweet Clutha's breast
That gorgeous stream where commerce never rests;
Upon whose banks I've oft distill'd the dews
Of fervent love, and pour'd on thee my muse,
That prince of rivers that joins the mighty sea
That's borne so many brave ships built by thee;
And will, I hope, yet bear a thousand more
With wealth and tidings to our Scottish shore.
Who would not love that stream, old Scotland's Clyde?
Oft have I watch'd its waters gently glide
Like infant angels o'er fair Shandon's beach,
Where thy dear master's princely mansion stretch
Its Gothic towers beneath the sun's bright rays—
The ancient emblem of departed days.
Oft have I wept in its surrounding woods
Where Gareloch gently rolls her silvery floods,
And sweetly echoes back o'er hill and plain
The monarch organ's sweet and deep-toned strain,
That fell like heavenly music on mine ears,
And filled my soul with thought of brighter spheres.
And I have seen that gorgeous window glass
Filled with the heroes of great mount Parnass—

Shakspeare, Milton, honoured Newton too,
Burns, Scott, and Goldsmith—Britain's authors true—
And many more brave and distinguished men,
Whose works for centuries yet will wear a gem.
Thy master's library contain a store
Num'rous as sands on Shandon's lovely shore.
 And who could dream I've wandered in those halls
Long ere the painters' hands adorned their walls;
That I have knelt and prayed within that place
Long ere the workman set with taste and grace
The rich enamelled China diamonds neat,
Which oft have kissed thy honoured master's feet.
This was my prayer—that he might live to see
His offspring's offspring all reach maturity.
This was my prayer—that his brave sons might be
The emblem of himself, noble and free,
And useful members through life's fleeting dream,
As their dear father many years has been.
That his gay mansion of such stately grace
May shield for centuries his own kindred race.
And thinkest thou this prayer will not avail,
Because 'twas breathed by woman weak and frail?
God listens to the weak as well's the strong,
And he may yet thy master's life prolong
To be a very aged honoured man;
Whose name and fame hath sailed to every land
Yet still thy dusty walls give joy to me
More pure than all the treasures of the sea.
Oh! what were all its wealth heaped mountains high
Could I no more thy towering dock descry?
If hills and mountains, oceans dark and blue,
Between us rolled to hide thee from my view.
 I would not leave thee, dear beloved place,
A crown, a sceptre, or a throne to grace;

To be a queen—the nation's flag unfurl—
A thousand times I'd be a Factory Girl!
To live near thee, and hear thy anvils clink,
And with thy sons that hard-won pleasure drink.
That joy that springs from wealth of daily toil,
Than be a queen sprung forth from royal soil.
Farewell, dear Work, the twilight hour is past,
Dark Luna's curtain o'er thy walls is cast;
Heaven's vaults distil their crystal dews,
Queen Venus waits to hail my midnight muse.
Farewell! Remember my best wish shall be
Thy master's welfare and success in thee.

My Mother.

She is—Oh! can I name her with a name—
    Too good, too great, too honoured for her worth;
What do I own that she dare not to claim?
    What gives me pleasure, fills her soul with mirth.

She is—Oh! what is she? Tall, handsome, fair,
    Prudent in all her ways, generous in heart;
One with whom there's few I can compare,
    One whose industry few can act a part.

She is—Oh! what is she? One that hath borne
    Trials and sorrows no language can express;
Still she looks fresh as summer's flowery morn,
    Although her cup overflows with bitterness.

She is—Oh! what is she? One that if dead,
    I might search the world and find no other
That could a radiance o'er this bosom spread
    Like her that gave me birth—my loving mother.

A Brother Poet.

In the still hour of night, when the world reposes,
    And the moon's silver beams on the mountains recline;
When the blue vaults of heaven their starlight discloses,
    Oh! thou art the bright star lights this bosom of mine.

Ah! never can language express the devotion
    Of my sisterly love and affection for thee;
Stern Time may roll on like the tide to the ocean,
    Yet thou never can'st know how dear thou'rt to me.

This is a gay world of beauty and splendour,
    And how vast are its riches on land and on sea;
But despite of its wealth and dazzling grandeur,
    It hath but one treasure in keeping for me.

And thou art that treasure, how dearly I prize thee,
    Thou'rt the theme of my muse still by night and by day;
Fame on her pages shall immortalise thee,
    Thy name shall yet live when thou sleep'st in the clay.

Yes, yes! I adore thee, thou gifted of heaven,
    Thy name round my heart is like ivy entwined;
Yes, thou art my chosen one whom God hath given
    The power of a genius in talent and mind.

Lines on the Death of a Beloved Child.

O God! Thy will be done; and who dare say
    Thou doest wrong? for all the earth is thine.
Thy will to give, Thy will to take away
    What is thine own; and yet I thought him mine.
        I thought him mine because I gave him birth,
        But, ah! he was too sweet to live on earth.

And thou didst call him home to dwell in heaven,
   For there alone will such as George be seen;
We seldom meet them in this world living,
   For soon they die and leave us like some dream—
     That filled our hearts with but one moment's gladness,
     Then wrecked our memory on the waves of sadness.

He was not ours, though fondly we adored him,
   And prized his beauty with our heart and soul;
He was not ours, though sadly we deplored him,
   And mourn him still with grief beyond control.
     He came from God, though in our bosoms nursed,
     He hath returned to whence he came at first.

His head, with curls fair of Nature's forming,
   Hung with rare beauty o'er his snowy brow;
His cheeks like rosebuds opening in the morning,
   Kissed with the dew-drop from some blossomed bough.
     His pearl teeth and lips of ruby hue,
     And beaming eyes of darkest violet blue.

He was the favourite of our little flock,
   Of all the five his beauty did excel;
And even yet I hear his well-known knock
   Come to the door and call on Isabel,
     William, or Malcolm to come out and play,
     And leave Eliza with mamma to stay.

When other children gathered in the court,
   We oft times watched him there amongst the rest;
While he performed his happy infant's sport,
   I've felt a heavenly joy thrill through my breast,
     And prayed to God that He might spare that one—
     My fairest favourite, and my youngest son.

And who could blame a mother's doting love?
   A father's fond affection for his son?
Who seemed more like an angel from above
   Than like an earth-born or a mortal one.
      He is immortal now—safe by the side
      Of his Almighty and immortal guide.

And, Ah! we little thought that death so soon
   Would strike the blow on our beloved boy;
And fill our happy home with darkest gloom,
   Bereaving us of many a hopeful joy.
      We could not think our boy, scarce in his bloom,
      Would leave us weeping o'er his early tomb.

But God is good, his mercy faileth never,
   Two daughters and two sons to us still live;
Had He not quell'd the fatal raging fever
   It might prevailed a greater loss to give.
      Then blessed be His high and holy name,
      He took but what he gave—His was the claim.

And may He give us strength and faith to bear
   Those disappointments oft'times fixed to life;
And when death comes to nip the thread of care,
   And end our sorrows in this world of strife,
      May He remove us to a better one,
      Where we in glory yet may meet our son.

The Maniac of the Green Wood.

I saw her when a little child,
   Her heart from care was free,
'Twining a wreath of May flowers wild
   Beneath a greenwood tree.

She wondered how they withered
   In her little hands so soon;
And fresh ones rose and gathered—
   They too withered in their bloom.

From a branch I saw her swinging,
   With the wreath upon her brow;
Then I heard her sweetly singing—
   I will go to mother now.

I will tell her that I made it;
   That by me alone 'twas done,
Down in the greenwood shaded
   From the hot and burning sun.

Ah! she knew not in these hours
   What ere long would be her doom;
That, just like her wreaths of flowers,
   She would wither in her bloom.

Then I saw her when a girl,
   Going gladly to the school;
And a bright and sunny curl
   Deck'd her features calm and cool.

On the way she was repeating
   The task that she had learned;
Her young heart with joy was beating—
   On her face no care discerned.

For her heart it knew no sorrow,
   Her doom was not in view;
To learn her task each morrow
   Was all the care she knew.

She dreamed not of the danger
   And the snares on woman's path;
To deceit she was a stranger,
   She had not yet felt its wrath.

Then I saw her when in womanhood,
    A fair and lovely flower;
She sat alone in yon greenwood,
    Beneath a shaded bower.

And she seemed as she was musing
    On some fair and lovely youth;
All his vows her thoughts confusing—
    Whether they were false or truth.

Ah! too true, she had been thinking
    Of her first and only love;
A sweet pleasure she was drinking
    That would soon a poison prove.

For those thoughts she deeply cherished
    The moment that I passed;
Ere long they would be perished
    In falsehood's bitter blast.

Then I heard her weeping sadly
    Within that same greenwood
Where I heard her singing gladly
    In days of her childhood.

No flowers she was gathering
    To wreath around her brow;
Her slender form was withering
    Like leaf on broken bow.

All youth's joys she had forgotten,
    In her memory they lay dead;
Her false lover's vows were broken,
    And her reason it was fled.

Poor girl! she was unshielded
    From the spoiler's perjury;
To a villain false she yielded—
    Now a maniac wild was she.

O'er a stream I saw her stooping
    To cool her fevered brow;
Then, wildly round her looking,
    She cried—'I see him now!'

'Ah! 'tis Henry; yes, I know him—
    That is the trysting tree;
And see how his tears are flowing—
    He sheds those tears for me.'

She had thought I was her lover,
    And called me by his name;
'Oh, heavens! do I recover
    My lost love back again?'

'Why, Henry, didst thou leave me?
    Why didst thou break thy vow?
Ah! 'twas cruel to deceive me!
    See I'm lost for ever now.'

Then I saw her prostrate lying;
    The look her features wore
Showed she was quickly dying,
    That she soon would be no more.

Then I heard her mother weeping,
    Her father breathe a prayer;
To Heaven he was entreating
    For his only child to spare.

Then she rose up from her pillow,
    Said 'weep no more for me;
For I soon will brave the billow
    Of death's dark raging sea.'

'Yea, I know that I am dying,
    I am insane no more;
And I hear a sweet voice crying—
    "Come to our happy shore."'

When these words she had spoken,
   She heaved a heavy sigh;
Life's golden cords had broken,
   Her soul had winged on high.

Kennedy's Dear Mill.

Oh! Kennedy's dear mill!
   To you I'll sing a song
For winter dark and dull;
   For another season's gone,
And summer's bright sunshine
   Thy little shed doth fill.
Prosperity is thine,
   Oh, Kennedy's dear mill!

'Tis not alone o'er thee
   Adversity hath passed,
For all the kingdoms three
   Hath felt its withering blast,
I shared thy better days,
   I also shared thine ill;
Now I hail hope's rays
   In Kennedy's dear mill.

Thou hast a secret spell
   For all as well as me;
Each girl loves thee well
   That ever wrought in thee.
They may leave thy blessed toil;
   But, find work they will,
They return back in a while
   To Kennedy's dear mill.

The girls so neat and fair,
    The boys so frank and free;
I see a charm that's rare
    In them as well as thee.
The sunlight of their smile
    Doth linger near me still,
And cheers me at my toil
    In Kennedy's dear mill.

And freedom's glorious shrine
    Is center'd in thy walls;
No tyrant knave to bind,
    No slavish chain enthrals.
The workers are as free
    As the sunshine on the hill;
Thy breath is liberty,
    Oh! Kennedy's dear mill.

We feel no coward fear
    When our dear master comes;
And when he's standing near,
    And gazing on our looms,
He hails us with a smile
    That is a brother's still,
No haughty lord of toil
    Owns Kennedy's dear mill.

Through Erin's vast commerce
    He bears a generous name;
And o'er the universe
    His praise I will proclaim.
When his workers are in grief,
    It is against his will;
He's the first to send relief
    From Kennedy's dear mill.

We will be happy yet,
    And bid all care adieu;
For we shall have a trip
    In another week or two.
And o'er in Bedford Street
    A happy band we will
In unity all meet
    At Kennedy's dear mill.

Now, Kennedy's dear mill,
    The best wish of my heart
Shall linger near you still,
    When from you I depart.
Whate'er my fate may be,
    Let me wander where I will,
Peace and prosperity
    To Kennedy's dear mill.

Childhood's Flowers.

THE GOWAN AND THE BUTTERCUP.

Oh! how I love those little flowers,
    They were the first I cherished;
Within my breast in childhood's hours
    With fond love they were nourished.

Upon the lovely banks of Clyde
    Many a wreath I've twined,
Until the setting sun would hide
    And leave me far behind.

Although the path was drear and dark
  That led me to my home,
Yet gay and cheerful as a lark
  There would I sport alone,

Singing with joy the childish muse
  That o'er my bosom stole;
Like infant buds kissed with the dews
  That gladden spring's bright soul.

I've twined a wreath around my brow,
  With bouquet in my breast;
Swift as an arrow from a bow
  The dewy grass I've press'd.
And through the lovely Glasgow Green
  I've quickly bent my way,
Through yon dark grove where fairy queen
  Dance in the moonlight ray.

No ghost I met in grove or green,
  But one my heart doth hate,
She was that powerful, partial queen,
  The world calls fickle fate.

She changed those happy childhood hours
  To years of grief and woe;
And in my breast in place of flowers
  She made rank weeds to grow.

She wreathed care clouds around my brow,
  And dim'd my once bright eyes;
Like blossoms blighted on a bough,
  She wrecked my hopes when high.

And now, alas! I roam no more
  Midst scenes of childhood's years,
I wander on a stranger shore,
  And feed its soil with tears.

Yet still I love those little flowers,
    Though weeds of gall are nurs'd
In this same breast where youthful hours
    Beheld them cherished first.

The Morning: A Recitation.

MOST RESPECTFULLY DEDICATED TO THE DUNDEE POWER-LOOM TENTERS' SPOUTING CLUB.

Hushed now are the rebels that fought in yon den,
Whose leading commanders were God-fearing men—
We hear not the echo from mountain and glen
    Of the Factory Boy's song in the morning!

In sackcloth and ashes his muse is laid low,
He feels his defeat and weeps now o'er his woe;
His sigh has the sound of a dastardly foe—
    He is seeking retreat in the morning!

And he wanders yon haunt of falsehood and guile,
Where wolves in sheep's clothing and hypocrites toil;
Where Love, Truth, and Virtue can ne'er again smile—
    For their glory hath gone with the morning!

It once was a garden both lovely and green,
And 'Genius' placed there a song-weaving queen;
But the false-hearted gardener, from motives unseen,
    Doomed her an outcast in the morning.

Like a storm-battered barque tossed on the sea,
A poor 'Factory Exile' she wandered Dundee;
Head-Tenters combined, at each committee—
    For to keep her at bay in the morning.

In an hour of her wildest sorrow of heart,
Ah! she sought for a balm to solace the smart;
But 'Gall of Infamy' was pour'd on the part—
    For to heal up her wounds in the morning!

No longer she's crying outside of its walls,
Her muse she is sighing in Chapelshade Halls;
Her voice, though still faint, unto memory recalls—
    She'll shine like a star in the morning!

When the withering blast of falsehood and shame
Shall crumble its strong walls and darken its fame;
The wormwood and nettle shall coil round its name—
    No flower shall e'er gladden its morning.

Like the ruins (of old) of Babylon's towers,
The cypress and willow shall weep in its bowers;
For a dark cloud of falsehood over it lowers—
    And a curse hovers there in the morning!

No flag of triumph waveth over its gate,
Nor guards of our city like sentinels wait
To guard from its rebels of malice and hate—
    Our poor Factory Exile in the morning!

Its old heirless owner is hastening away,
Where homage to mammon no longer he'll pay;
When his marrowless bones are mingled with clay—
    Then oblivion shall dawn o'er his morning.

Behold his new mansion! so stately and gay—
The boast of the ferry—looks down on the Tay;
But the ghost of a bankrupt, grim-like and grey—
    Wanders through its vast halls every morning!

The voice of his handmaids no longer we hear,
Like the growl of a lioness, burst on our ear;
In the local bard's column no longer appear—
    His Factory Boy's song in the morning.

The vengeance of Heaven hath smitten his lyre,
And the glory is dim of his poetic fire:
Now he fans no false flame his muse to inspire—
    For to brand us with shame in the morning!

No marvel his cheeks hath grown pale with regret,
The wrongs he hath done us he cannot forget;
And an old withered shrub of dark disrespect—
    It doth haunt his mind's eye every morning!

But the fame of that shrub immortal shall bloom,
When its old withered stem is wrapt in death's gloom;
Its blossoms of talent shall scatter perfume—
    O'er our Bonnie Dundee in the morning!

If the heavens send forth their glorious light
For to beam on our land of freedom and right;
The people shall know 'tis for justice we fight—
    We shall conquer or die in the Morning!

The Factory Exile.

Thou lovely verdant Factory! What binds my heart to thee?
Why art thou centered in my soul, twined round my memory?
Why dost thou hover o'er my dreams my slumbers to beguile?
When falsehood of the deepest dye has doomed me an Exile.

With tear-dimm'd eyes through fancy's veil I gaze upon thy
  walls;
Their bright enamelled golden tinge my bleeding heart enthrals,
I deem I am what once I was, still bending o'er my loom,
And musing on a lovely form of beauty's sweetest bloom.

The love-born joy that swells my soul, whilst I in fancy toil
Within thy much-loved walls again—where first I saw a
  smile
That I can never see again save with a sad regret;
Its sunny lustre now is lost in gloomy retrospect.

Ah, me! that one so beautiful should own so cruel a heart
As injure one who still to him did act a friendly part;
What have I done that he hath wrung my heart with bitter
  woe?
I was to him a faithful friend—Why has he grown my foe?

Language never can express how much I thought of him,
I prized his perseverance—so deep did I esteem
His active, energetic powers, his patience, and his worth:
Alas! I thought that he excell'd all other men on earth.

But God alone can only tell the base and cold reward
That he gave me in return for such a true regard;
He scattered thorns across my path, calumny o'er my name,
And crushed the blossoms of my hope—the laurels of my fame.

And God alone can only tell how I have been betrayed,
But vengeance unto Him belongs—then why am I dismayed?
Though I am tossing to and fro on sorrow's galling wave,
The persecuted findeth rest and peace beyond the grave.

Thou lovely, verdant Factory! though doom'd a poor exile—
Disgraced, degraded, never more within thy walls to toil,
I will forgive my enemies, though they have me belied,
And may the wrongs I bore in thee to me be sanctified.

The Absent Husband.

'Tis evening! The sun hath nigh sunk in the West,
And its last golden rays gilds the Tay's silver breast;
Whilst its waters flow onward to oceans afar,
I'll sing a love song to thee—Samuel Carr.

'Tis the wife of thy bosom—the loved of thy heart—
That doth now call upon thee her love to impart;
And with truth's golden fingers I'll strike Love's guitar,
And the theme of my muse shall be thee—Samuel Carr.

I am lonely and languid, my love, without thee,
Like to one that's forsaken I roam by the Dee;
But though distance divide us, death only can mar
My heart's deep communion with thee—Samuel Carr.

Ah! the river of Fidoch between us may flow,
And Craigellachie's mountains with heather-bells blow;
But no rivers or mountains can ever debar
Thy form from memory—my own Samuel Carr.

It is not thy beauty that in fancy I see,
For Nature did ne'er give that charm unto thee;
But thy fond, faithful heart is dearer by far
Than beauty's impression to me—Samuel Carr.

Though the stern breath of fate hath now blasted our hope,
Still my heart is unchanged—Love's spell yet unbroke—
For that dark 'Retrospect', it can never wage war,
With a guide for the future like thee—Samuel Carr.

O'er the Tay's silver bosom Night's curtain is flung,
Now my muse it is hushed, and my love song is sung;
And the young infant moon hails the bright evening star,
Fare-thee-well, my beloved one—adieu, Samuel Carr.

Welcome, Garibaldi.
A VOICE FROM DUNDEE.

Thou art welcome, Garibaldi! to Scotland's sweet Dundee,
Illustrious patriot warrior who set fair Italy free;
To slaves of Inquisition a balm thou didst impart,
And burst the galling fetters that bound thy nation's heart.

Thou art welcome, Garibaldi! unto our brown-heath soil,
To charm us with the beauty of thy bright and tranquil smile;
A king uncrowned, a conqueror, we truly know thou art,
Fame's diadem shines on thy brow, and glory jewels thy heart.

Thou art welcome, Garibaldi! where sons of freedom toil,
Ours may not be a land like thine, where sunshine ever smiles;
Ours is a land of liberty, where Freedom's flag belongs,
No slave is bowed beneath its yoke, no tyrant sings its songs.

Thou art welcome, Garibaldi! with all thy faithful train,
With heart and soul we hail thee, for freedom is thine aim;
No king did ever wear a crown nor hold a court levee
That we would make more welcome, brave warrior king, than thee.

Thou art welcome, Garibaldi! fair Italy's saving star;
Ah! we mourned thee as a brother, when thou from us afar
Lay prostrate on the lonely couch exhausted, pale and weak,
Disabled by a traitor's ball, but never by defeat.

Thou art welcome, Garibaldi! thou didst endure the pain,
It placed thy life in peril, yet deathless was its aim;
Napoleon's greedy eagles were hovering near thy grave,
But God decreed that thou wouldst live some other land to save.

Thou art welcome, Garibaldi! thou art the true-born type
Of our departed Wallace, who gained our country's right;
Defying every danger, he rushed amidst the strife,
And purchased Scotland's freedom with the ransom of his life.

Thou art welcome Garibaldi! hailed by one and all,
We'll give thee fare of cottage hearth, and feast of palace
    hall;
Old Scotland hath no honour that she would not give to thee,
Thou art beloved in all her lands as thou'rt in Dundee.

Thou art welcome, Garibaldi! across our far-famed Tay,
We'll lead thee to our Baxter Park, where flowers are bloom-
    ing gay;
The name of those who gave it, like thine own, can never die,
But live with fame immortal in a bright and cloudless sky.

Long life to Garibaldi! and when all thy warfare's done—
When thy task on earth is ended, and thy last victory won—
Oh, sweet shall be thy dreamless sleep, with angels for thy
    guard,
And a glorious crown in Heaven shall be thy rich reward.

Mourning for Garibaldi.

Oh, England! where now is thy fame-spreading story?
    Wrapt in a cloud of heart-bleeding shame;
And where's Garibaldi, that hero of glory,
    In whose love-fraught bosom you've planted a stain?

And where is the throne where thy sovereign is seated
    With the crown of royalty over her brow?
Can she deem for one moment we thus shall be cheated
    By her lords, dukes, and earls, who basely did bow

To a foreign despot, and his dastard dictations?
　　Oh! woe to thee England, the deed thou hast done
Shall brand thee for ever the meanest of nations;
　　Thou'st lost in one hour what in centuries was won.

And where are the banners thou proudly unfurled
　　When thy gay halls re-echoed that patriot's hymn?
Oh, England, thou once wert the 'gem' of the world,
　　But now is thy glory grown tarnished and dim.

Dost thou remember that thou wert in danger?
　　Though no Garibaldi had e'er trod thy soil;
For the eagle-eyed vulture could be thy avenger,
　　He thirsts for thy blood, oh! trust not his smile.

Though thou hast obeyed him, and sadly bereaved us
　　Of a hope which no language hath power to impart;
Though thy worthies conspired, and basely deceived us,
　　Garibaldi's dear form still dwells in our hearts.

Though we ne'er may behold him, his name we will cherish,
　　Our love-tears shall wash from his bosom thy shame;
And thy dastard insult ne'er in memory shall perish,
　　Thou hast snapt the gold link of our sister-wove chain.

Farewell, Garibaldi, though thou hast departed,
　　Torn from our hearts by Napoleon's base tools;
Know'st thou that old Scotland's a nation true hearted,
　　She ne'er shall be mocked by England's gay fools.

The Parting.

Farewell for ever, we must sever,
　　I am no longer loved by thee;
I have been true, but thou may'st rue,
　　The day thou didst prove false to me.

I thought the sun would cease to run
    His daily course around the sky,
Ere thou would'st prove a faithless lover,
    Or look on me with scornful eye.

Thy words were sweet when we did meet,
    I could not dream of secret guile,
Nor could I trace within thy face
    Deceit in thy dissembling smile.
This world's scorn is but a form—
    A fleeting phantom in my view,
I heed it not since thou hast brought
    A change o'er all the joys 1 knew.

Thou did'st impart joy to my heart,
    But now I feel the hope was vain;
'Twas but thy smile of treacherous guile
    That lighted up my dreaming brain.
I loved thee well; no tongue can tell
    The love I cherished up for thee;
I love thee still, despite thine ill,
    But Heaven alone my love shall see.

I will not blast the joy that's past,
    The happy hours I've spent with thee;
Nor yet estrange with deep revenge
    Thy love so falsely vowed to me.
Some chord may spring perchance to bring
    Thy memory back when first we meet;
Some conscious thought may mark the spot,
    And thou may'st feel some sad regret.

Some future hour of mystic power
    May bind thy mem'ry in a spell;
And thou may'st trace on time's iron face
    The wrongs that made my heart rebel.

My simple songs, my countless wrongs
    May swell before thee like a sea;
And thou may'st hate when it's too late
    All those that tried to injure me.

Perchance thy vow that's broken now,
    (All that on earth I once did cherish),
May come in dreams and midnight scenes,
    And waken guilt too strong to perish.
Adieu for ever! we must sever;
    Go. Thou art welcome, I am free;
Though falsehood's fame hath ting'd my name,
    Thou hast not proved its guilt in me.

The Workman for Ever.*

The Workman for ever, what rival can beat it?
    That casquet of talent worth treasures untold;
The Workman for ever, what power can defeat it?
    Such gems of the muse do its pages unfold.
And bards long departed in Death's silent slumbers
    Arise to our view like mountains of fame;
Their spirits unseen often gaze on its numbers,
    And heightens the valour of Scotland again.

The heroes of Scotland they gather around us
    In glorious armour that cannot grow dim;
We feel as their spell-blinding spirits had bound us,
    And fancy re-echoes the warrior's hymn.
We see Bannockburn lie expanding before us,
    Dyed dark with the patriot's red-reeking gore,
And we feel freedom's fire as wildly burst o'er us,
    As our forefathers did in the fam'd days of yore.

* The Workman, a Weekly Newspaper.

We see our brave Wallace the southern foes sweeping,
    Like leaves in brown autumn before him they fall;
We see our Sir Colin on Alma's heights greeting
    The slaves of a tyrant that strove to enthral;
And in fancy we gaze with swelling emotion
    On India's sun-soil thrice cursed with the blood
Of the sisters we loved, with tender devotion,
    Who sleep with their babes 'neath the dark rolling flood.

The scenes that we see in its poetic pages
    Shall waken a world of slumbering worth,
To burn like a beacon in forthcoming ages,
    When the poor man's pen hath jewell'd the earth.
Oh, Scotland! my country, thou boast of the world,
    For love, wit, and learning, for talent and song;
May the Workman's prize banner long be unfurled
    To gladden the hearths of thy working man's home.

The Lost Lover.

OH! do not ask me why I weep, nor bid me cease to sigh;
Say not the rose fades on my cheek, the violet in mine eye.
The fire of minstrelsy no more with song inspires my pen,
For I have lost my lover since he joined the riflemen.

He was the schoolmate of my youth, and when a 'prentice boy
He won this heart which he hath crushed and broken like a
    toy;
Our childhood years fled like a dream when rambling through
    the glen,
We heard no rumoured sound of war, no song of riflemen.

Stern fate with time rolls onward still like billows o'er the sea,
His heart that now seems cold and strange was long since
    pledged to me;
No more we roam sweet Clutha's banks as we did wander then,
Those golden joys have perished since he joined the riflemen.

The rifles are a gallant corps, their scientific art
Shall make them noble soldiers, warriors to a mark;
To do or die is their resolve, no matter where or when,
The safe-guards of our city still we'll find our riflemen.

To fight for love and liberty is their spontaneous aim,
That Britain's banners still may wave on towers of golden fame;
The sons of independent toil, the theme of poet's pen,
The hopes of every free-born heart are our brave riflemen.

The Queen has many armies, her nations to protect,
And if I were her daughter fair with freedom to elect,
The husband of my own heart's choice I'd place my diadem,
Beneath the feet of him I love amongst the riflemen.

The Suicide.

Oh, night! how beautiful a t thou?
    Thy young queen brightly beaming;
A starry coronet on her brow,
    With jewell'd pearls gleaming.
How sweet and balmy is the breeze
    Which thou art gently flinging?
It whispers through the forest trees
    Like infant angels singing.

My false love on the banks of Tay
  Is silently reposing;
Scenes of a brighter, better day
  His dreams are now disclosing—
He dreams not of the raging strife
  That's in my bosom swelling,
That her he pledged would be his wife
  Is dying near his dwelling.

Life is a lasting grief to me—
  A chain of endless sadness;
Its galling cup of misery
  I've drained, yea, unto madness.
Oh night! how beautiful art thou?
  How calm thy breeze is blowing?
Those drops that gather on my brow
  Are tears from angels flowing.

To-morrow thou shalt come again,
  Thy queen in regal brightness,
Follow'd by her starry train,
  And lamps of gorgeous lightness.
But never shall my tear-dimm'd eyes
  In this wide world behold thee;
Long ere the sun doth light the skies,
  Death's cold arms shall enfold me.

Here lies within this fatal cup
  What soon will end my weeping;
Farewell, false love, I've drank it up,
  Ere long I will be sleeping.
Oh, night! how beautiful thou art?
  Thy sparkling beauty numbers
The scorching pangs that burn this heart—
  Oh! welcome death's sweet slumbers.

Love Outwitted.

As youthful love one day was straying,
    He stole into a rosy bower,
Where Genius sat her time betraying
    Musing on a fragrant flower.

She was handsome, young, and pretty;
    Sweeter was she than the flower;
And soft and soothing was the ditty
    That o'er its blossoms she did pour.

Like a thief he stole behind her,
    Fear'd lest she might him descry,
And in his golden chains to bind her,
    He this artful plan did try.

A rose tree o'er her head was bending,
    With fragrance sweet this tree was fraught;
He climb'd it, from it hung suspending,
    That in her arms he might be caught.

She quickly started from her musing,
    And caught him gently in her arms,
The struggle all her robes confusing,
    Displayed her bosom's snowy charms.

Art thou injured, lovely creature?
    Let me hold thee to my heart;
And while he gazed upon each feature,
    Into her breast he plunged his dart.

Lovely genius, long I've sought thee,
    Nor have I sought thee all in vain;
With life's peril I have bought thee,
    And we must never part again.

Lovely genius, scientific,
    Where is the heart you cannot move?
Friend of patriot and politic,
    Sometimes both friend and foe to love.

While thus he spoke his chains he heaved
    Round her young and happy heart;
The links and knots he firmly weaved,
    Defying skill to burst apart.

Genius looked not melancholy,
    Nor showed that she his chains defied;
But to deceive him in his folly,
    Next her artful plan she tried.

Soon his boastings I will scatter,
    His hopes I'll prostrate in decay,
Unlink each knot while him I flatter,
    Then laugh at him and fly away.

Thus she then began her ditty,
    Soft and sad-like was its strain;
'Ah! poor love I do thee pity,
    Thine has been a matchless pain

'Oh, love! thou art the golden light
    That leads us to the path of hope,
And cheers us on through sorrow's night,
    While thus she said she loosed a knot.

'Oh, love! thou art a secret chain,
    The sigh of sorrow thou canst smother;
Though oft you lead us to do harm,
    While thus she said she loosed another.

'Oh, love! that I had sooner met thee,
    This heart of mine had ne'er been sore;
Now with pleasure I'll accept thee,
    While thus she said she loosed four.

'Oh, love! thou art an angel pensive,
    A halo round our heads to cast;
Few to wisdom are so sensive,
    While thus she said she loosed the last.

'Oh, love! thou art a foolish knave
    To give thyself such fruitless pain,
To deem that I would be thy slave,
    Then cast at him his golden chain.

'Fool, presumption, type of folly,
    I leave thee thy rash deed to rue,
To cast thy chains round melancholy—
    Good-bye, my love,' then off she flew.

The Happy Man.

Laugh on, laugh on! thou happy man, while life is young and bright,
For it is not in old withered age that man can find delight;
Laugh on—and be what thou hast been—and when that thou art gone,
Thy memory will be cherished in records yet unknown.

Deem not though fate hath sever'd us and torn thy love apart,
That the love I cherished once for thee is withered in my heart;
It lives in records of thy praise, and bloometh still as sweet,
And safe as misers hoard their gold within its secret keep.

Like the miser I'll not give it up until you change your life,
Till once I see whom thou dost choose to be thy loving wife;
Then I will know my love is lost, that hope hath flattered me,
And thou shalt read in those records how true I've loved thee.

Though falsehood and misfortune hath made me what I am,
Could you deem me so ungrateful as not to love the man
Who did befriend me in that hour when no other friend was
    near—
Who brought consolation to my heart and dried the bitter
    tear?

Yes, thou wert to me a friend in need, and I will ne'er forget
What thou hast done for me and mine—I may reward thee yet;
My grandsire slumbers with the dead—to him thou wert a
    son—
And thy mother she was dutiful to that departed one.

But those are not the secret ties that bind me unto thee,
I've searched thee long and found thee out all that a man
    can be;
Thou makest peace and mendest strife where discord overflows
And thy hand is ever stretched to aid where hunger over-
    throws.

When in my young and thoughtless years fair beauty was
    my pride,
I mused upon it day and night, and longed to be its bride.
Now, I feel the man is worth a world who acts a generous
    part,
And a paradise of beauty is centered in thy heart.

For thou art just and generous, candid and sincere,
A man whose truth and confidence could stand a thousand
    year;

Thy merry tales may be of lies, thy jokes look foolish like,
But 'take thee,' 'take thee,' all in all, thou art a man upright.

Though fate hath brought a change o'er me, still I have lovers yet;
But still, amidst their flattering praise, I cannot thee forget,
For thou, my philanthropic friend, comes so near, so dear to me.
Can you tell me, happy laughing man! why I think so much of thee?

'Tis not alone by light of day that I do think of thee,
For in the lonely midnight hour still thou art there with me!
And the dreams of sweet delusion that wanders through my brain—
They waken me to madness that words can never name.

Laugh on, laugh on! thou happy man, desponding hearts to cheer,
Oh! who could feel a sorrow if thou wert only near;
Yea, many time thy merry laugh hath soothed my cares to rest,
And pour'd a healing balm upon my bleeding burning breast.

The Rifleman's Melody.

They say the French are coming, boys!
To fight on Britain's shore;
With blood to stain her freeman's plain,
And soak her fields with gore.

Give them a hearty welcome, boys,
　　And let them feel the power
Of British might before they fight
　　Her sons a half-an-hour.

She conquered Bonaparte, my boys—
　　Defeated Nicholas, too;
She's already waiting, boys,
　　Napoleon to subdue.
The glorious fire of freedom
　　Is burning in her heart;
So, let the French dogs come, my boys,
　　She fears no mastiff's bark.

Enshrined within the tomb, my boys,
　　Departed heroes lie,
And spirits of the martyr'd dead
　　That live beyond the sky
Inspire each British heart, my boys,
　　That burns for French defeat;
So, let the bloodhounds come, my boys,
　　She fears no dastard's threat.

Her banners are red, white, and blue,
　　The standard flag of yore,
When noble William Wallace rode
　　Deep in the Saxon's gore.
And while she sings that patriot's hymn,
　　Where freedom's banner waves,
Shall French usurpers claim her rights,
　　And make her freemen slaves.

By Heaven, we love our home, boys,
　　With love that is sincere;
But we love the breath of freedom,
　　It is to us more dear.

And whilst our arms can draw the sword
    Our willing aid to lend,
Like ' Wallace Wight ' we'll sternly fight
    Our country to defend.

Arise! the French are coming, boys,
    And let our watchword be—
To conquer or to die, my boys,
    For Britain shall be free.
And when that they arrive, my boys,
    We soon shall let them feel,
Our love of right shall aid with might
    Our swords of British steel.

Love and War.

FAREWELL, my warlike lover now! a long farewell to thee,
Thy war-worn soul hath winged its flight where I no more shall see
Thy form so fair, whose faithful heart was constant as the sun,
To her that sadly wails thee now, thou dear departed one.

I saw thee weep when last we met, thy tears in secret fell;
How could love make a warrior weep if he had not loved well?
I heard thy bosom's bursting sighs when parting from thy side,
The fragrance of their balmy breath were honour, truth, and pride.

I see thee now in all my thoughts, yes—yes in every dream
Thou dost haunt me like a vision in every living scene;
I see thy broad and manly breast heave forth the same deep sighs;
I see the same hot burning tears roll from thy tear-dimm'd eyes.

I see thee sadly gaze around, and in thy every look
I read the language of thy heart like pages of a book;
I see a dark cloud on thy brow—the shadow of regret,
For thou art gazing, Walter, on the place where first we met.

Methinks I hear the trumpet sound the word of war's command;
I hear thee tell thy prancing steed in steadiness to stand;
Thy quivering lips they move apart, methinks to breath my name;
A voice from Heaven whispers thee that thou shalt soon be slain.

The camp is hushed. I see thee draw a locket from thy breast;
I see a lovely golden ring unto thy pale lips pressed;
I see thee give them unto one, and thy sad looks can tell
Thou givest them as a token of thy last and long farewell.

I see thee on the battle-field amidst our allies brave;
I see thee fall where thousands fell, and none thy life can save;
I see thee rudely trampled down where I dare not to come,
To heave one sigh or drop a tear o'er my you g warrior's tomb.

I see a war-steed bounding through amidst the battle fray,
Like uncaged bird on freedom's wings it swiftly flies away;
The blood is flowing from its side as wildly on it flies,
And, neighing loudly, turns to gaze where its dead master lies.

I see the 'quarrys' taken, the 'mameleon' hurled down;
I hear them shout for England and Scotland's old renown;
I see a river flowing, 'tis the precious stream of life,
That leaves the helpless orphan and the hapless widow'd wife.

I see thee, then, in all that's fair, or beautiful and bright;
I see thee in the jewell'd star that hails the morning light;
I see thee through the azure sky when lowering clouds are shriven,
Seated near the glorious throne—a soldier brave of Heaven.

Then, methinks, the war is ended—all strife and carnage done—
That Britain's sons hath gained the day—Sebastopol is won.
Upon each ruined fortress height fair Britain's flag waves free,
Unto our gallant allies brave belongs the victory.

But thou, my warlike lover, now liest numbered with the dead;
The laurels of thy country's love are wreathed around thy head;
Thy name shall be immortalised in records of the brave,
Who, for their Queen and country, died and found an honour'd grave.

A Mother's Love.*

I LOVE thee, I love thee, and life will depart
Ere thy mother forgets thee, sweet child of her heart;
Yea, death's shadows only my memory can dim,
For thou'rt dearer than life to me—Mary Achin.

I love thee, I love thee, and six years hath now fled
Since first on my bosom I pillow'd thy head;
Since I first did behold thee in sorrow and sin,
Thou sweet offspring of false love—my Mary Achin.

I love thee, I love thee, and twelve months hath now past,
My sweet child, since I gazed on thy fairy form last;
And our parting brought sorrow, known only to Him
Who can see through the heart's depths—my Mary Achin.

I love thee, I love thee, oh! when shalt thou rest
Thy sweet angel face on this heart-burning breast;
Thy last parting kiss lingers still on my chin,
Embalmed with a blessing from Mary Achin.

* Written for Miss Mary Achenvole. Born, 14th September, 1852.
Written in Belfast, 1858.

I love thee, I love thee, thy beauty and youth
Are spotless and pure as the fountain of truth;
Thou'rt my star in the night, till daybreak begin,
And my sunshine by noontide—my Mary Achin.

I love thee, I love thee, wherever I go
Thou'rt shrined in my bosom in joy or in woe;
A murmuring music my fancy doth win,
'Tis the voice of my darling—Mary Achin.

I love thee, I love thee, is ever my lay,
I sigh it by night and I sing it by day,
Its chorus swells forth like the stern patriot's hymn,
Thrice hallowed with visions of Mary Achin.

I love thee, I love thee, though now far away
Thou'rt nearer and dearer to me every day;
Would they give me my choice—a nation to win—
I would not exchange with my Mary Achin.

To my Aunt Phemie.

DEAR AUNT, the thoughts of bygone years rush wildly o'er my brain—
I strive to stay their swelling tide, but, ah! it is in vain;
Those innocent and gladsome hours that I have spent with thee,
Above all other after-scenes, float still on memory.

And thou wert young and handsome then—a woman in thy prime;
Thy cheeks wore not what they now wear—the dark impress of time.

Whilst o'er my brow my mother shed my hair's bright sunny wave,
Then wouldst thou speak of him that sleeps far in a foreign grave.

Time on his iron pinions fled, and parted thee and me,
Then came the news that thou hadst wed a husband in Dundee.
When flowing plenty cheered thy home, and joy around thee smiled,
One heart was sad within the home where Ellen was beguiled.

Glad nature swelled my soul with song, my brow was wreathed with fame,
Our Royal Sovereign read my muse, and praised my gifted name;
But like the leaves which autumn winds do scatter to and fro,
The withering breath of false love came and laid hope's blossoms low.

'Twas well my future fate was veiled from youth's bright golden view;
I had the name of many friends, yet friends I had but few;
For those that measured all my faults, considered not my wrongs—
I've wept in secret solitude whilst others sung my songs.

Twelve silvery moons had jewell'd the sky, the stars with diamond ray
Had gemm'd the dew from Heaven's vaults upon my mother's clay;
No parent link to bind to earth, no house nor hearth for me—
An orphan wrapt in mourning weeds I came unto Dundee.

And Heaven alone can only tell my hardships in that land;
Many a time I've passed thy door whilst thou at it did'st stand;

When I was weary wandering, friendless, cold, and weak,
Oh God, I've passed my own aunt by, yet could not, dare not speak.

And seventeen bright summer suns far in the west had set
Since thou and I had parted first, and thus on Tay's banks met;
Till death my tear-dimm'd eyes doth close, I'll ne'er forget the look
Of haughty scorn thou gavest me—thy cold and stern rebuke.

Dear aunt, thy heart is changed now—some spell has thee beguil'd,
Or thou wouldst ne'er have turned thy back upon thy brother's child;
For couldst thou think as I have thought, and feel as I have felt,
Yea, though thy heart was adamant, my name that heart might melt.

An Appeal.[*]

O TAKE me, take me with you, thou noble warlike corps!
Must I be sever'd from you, to see you never more?
Heavens! leave me not behind: from you I cannot part;
Ten thousand stinging adders are wreath'd around my heart.

O take me, take me with you, thou noble warlike band!
I'll pledge my truth and honour, my life, my heart and hand,
Amongst your wives and children a servant's work to do,
Ever kind and willing unto one and all of you.

[*] Written in Belfast on the departure of the Sappers and Miners for Newry, 1858.

O take me, take me with you! O tell me what I've done,
That any man amongst you has cause my name to shun!
I have loved you all alike, and dreamt upon your fame,
And my heart doth swell with pleasure to hear a Sapper's name.

O take me, take me with you! Ah, do not leave me here!
Awake your hearts to pity, for the evil hour is near!
Can you forsake a woman that lives but to adore
The name, the fame, and honour of your gay gallant corps?

O take me, take me with you! I'll pass through fire and flood,
Share thy fates in peaceful home or battle-field of blood;
For a strange and mystic spell has bound you to my soul—
A mysterious fascination death can alone control.

O take me, take me with you! Heed not what people say!
Condemn me not until you try, then judge me as you may;
Many speak ill of me, I know, I've borne a thousand wrongs;
I am hated not for my faults, but envied for my songs.

O take me, take me with you! I'll call upon my muse,
Thy names in songs of glory together I'll infuse;
And mine shall be a history—a Factory Girl's romance—
A truth more strange than fiction, and not of random chance.

Lovely Johnie White.
WRITTEN BY THE REQUEST OF A YOUNG LADY.

O HUSH, thou whispering summer breeze, and listen to me now,
For love has tempted me again to break a solemn vow;
For I have met a lovely youth whose dazzling beauty bright,
Has bound me in a mystic spell, they call him Johnie White.

Young Johnie is a merchant's son, out in the —— Road,
His is the rustic beauty that was form'd by nature's God;
No cold contempt contracts his smile, no proud assuming might
Doth sway the young and gentle heart of lovely Johnie White.

His is the true-born beauty that powerfully displays
That nature unadorn'd with pride shown in its simplest ways—
A beauty that is hallowed with Heaven's own love-born light;
Such is the witching beauty God has given to Johnie White.

No empty pride, no haughty scorn dwells in young Johnie's
    breast,
But a look that's loved and loving upon his face doth rest;
And when he smiles, his bright blue eyes send forth a world
    of light,
And shadow melts to sunshine beside young Johnie White.

His brow, like polish'd marble, shines beautiful and fair;
His beaming eyes of azure blue give him a look that's rare;
His cheeks are like the blooming rose that ne'er felt autumn's
    blight—
O, who could gaze upon him and not love Johnie White?

His father and his mother, his sister and a friend,
Did meet one night together some happy hours to spend;
If e'er I felt a heaven on earth, I'm sure it was that night,
With our little pic-nic party, myself, and Johnie White.

Young Johnie sang a lovely song that's called 'The Broken
    Spell,'
Of gathering shells from youth till age doth answer death's
    dark knell;
I wish that Heaven would break the spell that's bound me in
    its might,
Or bind me ere the spell is broke to lovely Johnie White.

Blow now, thou balmy summer breeze, and cool my burning brow,
For I feel in stern reality I never loved till now;
And though I lived a thousand years, I ne'er would seek to write
Upon a fairer, sweeter youth than lovely Johnie White.

Farewell.
WRITTEN BY REQUEST.

Farewell, false one, my sun of joy has set
   Within the grave of sad and silent grief;
We yet may meet, but not as we have met,
   No more thy smiles can bring my heart relief.
It would been better far I ne'er had known
Such hopes and joys when they were not my own.

But sad and hopeless though my heart may be,
   Still I have vow'd to love thee none the less,
For thou art all that once brought joy to me,
   Now thou art all that brings me wretchedness.
Yet still I love and prize thy very name,
Though broken trust doth brand thy brow with shame.

What is this gay green world unto me now?
   A weary waste, a dark and lonesome void.
Hope's golden star that shone upon my brow
   Shines on the bosom of thy new made bride.
Ah! may she prove a true and loving wife;
May with'ring care ne'er blight her future life.

And when you fold her to thy perjured heart,
   And gaze with gladness on her angel face,
Ah! think of her whose smiles did joy impart
   Long ere her wealth had charm'd thee with its grace.
Let memory mark thy every selfish thought
That all thy joys are with my misery bought.

Lines to a Lovely Youth,
A BOATBUILDER) LEAVING THE TOWN.

O LEAVE me not, because I love thee well!
    Could woman look on thee and not feel love?
Ah! thou hast bound me in thy beauty's spell,
    And made each chord within my heart to move,
As if some love-inspiring charm were given
To tune my soul with melodies of Heaven.

O who could gaze upon thy handsome form,
    And meet those glances of such starlight brightness,
Thy glowing cheeks, like rose of summer's morn,
    Thy ruby lips, and teeth of pearly whiteness—
O who could look on such a form as thine
And feel no love around her bosom twine?

And thou art brave as thou art beautiful—
    'Tis not in beauty thou alone excel;
And thou art ever kind and dutiful.
    By young and old thou art beloved well,
And thou hast won each village maiden's heart—
Emblem of beauty, prince of nature's art!

No lowland youth hath roam'd the banks of Clyde
    With half thy masculine majesty or grace;
And when you roam to watch the evening tide,
    Each maiden sighs while gazing on thy face;
Each gallant ship upon whose deck you stand
Doth bear thy vision to a foreign land.

O could the mountains of thy Highland home
    But breathe thy name would they not call thee back.
And bid thee here no longer now to roam,
    But to return and chase the wild deer's track;

To leave a joy where'er thy footsteps fell,
On mountain daisy or blue heather bell.

O how young beauty's queen would fly to meet thee,
  And fold thee in her mantle of sweet green,
And there each lovely flower would spring to greet thee,
  And kiss thy feet amidst their rosy sheen.
Each little bird with songs of joyful mirth
Would welcome thee back to thy place of birth.

But who, alas! will cheer my drooping heart?
  Ah! who to me hope's banner will unfurl?
No other smile can e'er a charm impart
  To the lone bosom of 'The Factory Girl.'
If thou dost leave me here in grief forlorn,
My golden dreams are from my bosom torn.

O leave me not because I love thee well;
  Could woman look on thee and not feel love?
Ah! thou hast bound me in thy beauty's spell,
  And made each chord within my heart to move
As if some love-born charm to me was given
To string my harp with melodies of Heaven.

Lines

MOST RESPECTFULLY DEDICATED TO MR AND MRS BROWN.

There is beauty in the sunlight that soars the summer sky,
There is beauty on the broad blue sea to greet the poet's eye,
But beauty richer far than those thy bosoms doth impart,
That heals my sick soul's bleeding woes and cheers my drooping
    heart.

It is a beauty richer far than all the gems on earth,
It's brighter than the morning star which Heaven did give birth,
It is thy hearts of tender love which other's woes can melt,
And hands that can as truly prove that sympathy was felt.

May Heaven bless the loving pair which Heaven hath mated well,
Though bleeding grief and death-eyed care now in thy household dwell,
Though now thy lovely Margaret's dead and from thy bosom shriven,
'Tis sweet to know her soul hath fled an angel fair of Heaven

And may thy dear Elizabeth, so full of lively glee,
Be to thy home a love-born gift, in fancy mild and free;
And may thy dear young Isabel, so pensive, sweet, and mild,
Be spared in beauty to excel—on her fair genius smiled.

May John be like the opening rose, that 'gem' of nature's plan,
Should he his manhood leaves unclose, still be a useful man;
May little Daniel still revive in glowing life and health,
He is the flower of all the five, and worth a world's wealth.

Whate'er thy children's looks appear, whate'er their deeds impart,
May they be like their parents dear, still own a generous heart,
Thy kindness did my woes becalm, and now the name of Brown
Shall be unto my heart a balm, unto my head a crown.

Accept my blessing, dearest friends, that I devote to thee,
My grateful prayer to thee extends unto eternity;
I'll think of thee where'er I roam through life's path, calm or rude,
Although near thee I may not come, I'll still feel gratitude.

The Broken Heart.
A TALE.

Ah! he sought not the mountain, he sought not the vale,
Nor sought he the greenwood or the heath cover'd dale,
Nor sought he the dew-spangled fair flowery lea,
Where with her he once lov'd he had wander'd so free,
Far excluded from joy where bright hope cast no rays,
Ah! this youth often hid from his fellow-man's gaze,
Like a young timid bird when it first leaves its nest,
Then returns fraught with fear to its fond mother's breast.
So sought he the lonely and the dark hiding place
Where no eye but his God's his deep sorrow could trace,
For his solace was solitude mingled with grief,
And the still cup of death could alone bring relief.

Yet 'tis strange that he felt not one wish for to cast
A farewell 'halo' around the joys of the past.
From that hour dark falsehood had first sealed his fate,
All the scenes he once loved he now seemed to hate;
But he hated them not, though he would not go back
To chase the wild fawn o'er the mountain's rude track,
And muse on fair nature the solace of song,
For he was a genius who had felt all this wrong;
And he would not go back, when an injured one,
To gaze on the flowers that smil'd sweet to the sun,
Whose pure spotless bosoms were so free from the stain
Of that fair but false bosom that caus'd all his pain.

Ah! he shrunk from the gaze of the heath mountain's brow,
For 'twas there that his false love had first breath'd her vow.
Though his heart it recoiled at what she had done,
Yet he loved her still though a false perjur'd one;

And his home of gay splendour no pleasure could bring
To his heart that was poison'd with perjury's sting.
Friends loved to mock him in the midst of his grief,
But he sought not their pity nor yet their relief;
But he left them for ever to wander alone
Till the message of Death would summon him home
To that sweet land of rest, the traveller's last bourne,
Whence he never again can to sorrow return.

How calm and resigned was this youth to his doom,
When he wept it was not o'er his hope's blighted bloom,
When he sighed it was not that it was too late
To retrieve his too hopeless or sorrowful fate;
But he had been wrong'd by a vow rashly given,
And his love it was pure and spotless as Heaven.
Often times have I trac'd him to where he would dwell,
In some dark lonely cave or a cold silent cell.
Yea, though joy from his bosom had taken its flight,
Still he was my hope-star of radiance so bright,
For I lov'd him full well though he lov'd another—
He was dearer, by far, to me than a brother.

The last time I saw him he was wand'ring alone;
No doubt he was musing o'er the joys that were gone,
For I saw the large tears falling fast from his eyes
As he gaz'd on the ground, then look'd up to the skies;
And clasping his hand on his pale, fever'd brow,
He cried wildly 'O God, where are those joys now?'
Then the burning anguish that in heaps were piled
In his heart-bleeding bosom burst in fury wild
From his sunk languid eyes of a fierce dragon flame,
And he heard me not when I called out his name,
But he gazed on a ring of dark auburn hair
That his false love had given as a pledge to wear.

On a bright golden clasp was engraven her name
Who had broken his young heart and blasted his fame.
He kissed it and blessed her that had done him the ill,
Then he cried 'O my God, I love, love her still,
And O guard her, kind Heaven, from falsehood's vile blast,
For she was my first love and she shall be my last.

Then he wandered away to the High Churchyard,
And I follow'd him still with a sister's regard,
(And Oh where is the heart that could remain unmoved
In an hour such as this, though it ne'er had lov'd?)
Then he laid himself down on a cold damp grave,
And I listen'd—oh, horror! he began to rave,
For she whom his soul's love to madness had nursed.
O'er and o'er again still I heard her thus cursed.
Yea, cursed, and those curses—O deem it not strange—
Had availed in the heavens with just revenge,
For on that very night, nay, that very same hour,
When the clock tolled twelve from the High Church tower,
She—that heart-breaking beauty of this world of breath—
Became food for the worms in the world of death.
Ah! that was the hour I heard him thus rave,
And in wild agony writhe on the cold damp grave.

The skies were cloudless, and the moon it shone bright,
I alone with a maniac in that hour of midnight.
All alone! Oh, no, for bright spirits they were nigh
For to waft his dear soul unto regions on high.
When he grew more calm he had ceased for to speak,
And I thought he had worn himself o'er to sleep.
With a sad aching heart and a wild anxious ear
Then I ventur'd to draw me more near and still near,
Till I bent o'er his pale yet still lovely young face,
In the bright moonbeams there all its beauty to trace.

With trembling hands I then raised his dear head:
O merciful heavens, I had kissed the dead!
And its touch! Ah! methinks that I feel even now.
Yet this sad fate was mine, and I cannot tell how;
But I loved him too well then to fly away,
And desert his remains, although cold lifeless clay.
Yes, those lips I had pressed were the lips of the dead.
Ah! the cold clay was there, but the spirit had fled.
Yes, fled to a world where sad sorrow's dart
Cannot enter the bosom to break the young heart.

On the Loss of the Dalhousie.

Ah! soundly they sleep 'neath the waters deep,
    Of our lovely but treacherous Tay;
In the dead of night they have taken flight
    To sleep 'neath its silvery spray.
Life's voyage is o'er and death's sails unfurl'd,
And we hope they've gain'd a brighter world.

Ah! soundly they sleep 'neath the waters deep,
    And hushed are the angry waves,
For the tyrant storm hath now wrapt each form
    In their cold and watery graves;
And the sea nymphs crowd on the shattered deck
To weep pearl tears o'er the life-lost wreck.

Ah! soundly they sleep 'neath the waters deep,
    None are left the sad tale to tell,
When the boiling surge sung their last death dirge,
    And the wild raging sea did swell,
And sunk in its wrath the proud noble boat
That oft o'er our glorious Tay did float.

Ah! soundly they sleep 'neath the waters deep,
    And never again will return
To gladden with mirth each sad desolate hearth,
    Where their widows and orphans mourn.
Ah! in vain are their sad unavailing tears,
Their heartrending sighs cannot greet their ears.

O God of Heaven! thou who hast given
    Thy promise of mercy still sure
To succour the life of the widow'd wife,
    And food for the orphans procure.
Yea, bid thou thine Angel of Love to come,
And light up with her smile their cheerless home.

Let thy will be done thou most holy 'One,'
    Thou hast taken but what thou gave;
They were all thine own which thou did'st call home
    For to sleep in an ocean grave.
When thou call'st them hence from their dark abode,
May it be to dwell in Heaven, O God!

The Summer's Away.

Sun-eyed, flower-gem'd summer, hath sweetly passed away,
And sallow autumn's chilling breath foretells dark winter's day;
Glad nature once so beautiful weeps wildly o'er her wane,
Her murmuring mingles with the blast that howls across the main.

Ah! has she like a spirit bright fled far beyond the skies?
Or sleeps she in the silent soil, in spring time to arise,
And spangle with her silver beams the dew-kiss'd infant flower,
And gladden with her sunny smiles the ivy-woven bower?

Yea, though a hazy veil enshroud the azure skies above,
Fair summer will return again adorn'd in robes of love,
Followed by her flowery train with fragrant breath sublime,
She'll blow the budding roses forth that crown the summer time.
    Mankind like summer on this earth but for a season bloom,
    Then like her flowers he fades away to dust within the tomb.

The Drunkard's Wife.*

WELL I remember when I first saw thee, Hannah,
Thou wert sweet as the rose—fair as Diana;
And thy brow like the marble was shining and fair,
Richly deck'd with thy ringlets of bright auburn hair.

Thou wert lovely and loving—beloved by all—
Young and old smil'd to greet thee at banquet and ball;
Thy teeth were like pearls of the deep ocean grave,
Neatly set in the mouth of a pure coral cave.

Thy voice was the sweet'st that swell'd through the hall—
Like some soft, fairy lute on our ears it did fall;
Thy step was the light'st in the gay promenade,
And the young men all thought thee a beautiful maid.

But the cold-hearted spoiler—ah! woe be his doom—
To blight such a flower in the pride of its bloom;
Like a thief in the night he stole to thy bower,
And the dew of rank poison down on thee did shower.

Ah! his words they were sweet, and thy heart it was young,
And dream'd not that poison slept under his tongue;

* Written on my mother's youngest sister, whose history falls little short of the picture painted by my humble pen.—E. J.

He knew thou didst love him, and thy fair hand he press'd,
Then thou gav'st him the heart that beat high in thy breast.

Ah! how chang'd now the scenes from those once happy years,
For sweet songs you give sighs, and for smiles you give tears.
Now the dark cup of sorrow embitters thy life,
To a hard hearted drunkard, ah! thou art a wife.

And thy face, once so lovely, is sallow and pale
As the sun-sicken'd lily that droops in the vale;
And thy cheeks, once like roses, are wash'd white with tears,
Yea, thou look'st like to one that is furrow'd with years.

O'er thy brow once so bright a dark care cloud is cast,
And no trace can we find of the beauty that's past;
Thine eyes have grown hollow and so death-like to view—
They have lost all their lustre of bright azure blue.

And thy tall slender form is nigh bent to the ground,
And thy voice hath lost all its sweet musical sound,
And the pale face of famine looks forth in despair,
Through the torn, tatter'd garments thou'rt doom'd now to wear.

Ah! poor Hannah, thou once wert the pride of our land,
And how worthy the wooers that sought thy fair hand?
But their love to thy bosom no joy could impart—
It was falsehood and beauty that won thy young heart.

When I look on thee now, and think what thou hast been,
When thy young hopes, unclouded, flew on like a dream—
When I see thee a victim by drunkenness curs'd,
Mem'ry seems but a phantom that fancy hath nursed.

And that child which so fondly thou hold'st to thy breast,
Unconscious of woe, it now slumbers at rest;
Should it live unto manhood, like its father to turn,
Ah! far better for thee it were laid 'neath the urn.

For its father's a drunkard! The lone hours of night
Beholds thee, poor Hannah, sit trembling with fright,
And the weak dying embers to ashes decay,
Whilst thou wait on his coming till dawning of day.

Alas! wretched Hannah, how I feel for thy woes,
And I long to behold thee in peaceful repose,
For thy heart wears a history of heartrending strife,
But death will soon release thee, thou poor drunkard's wife!

Address
TO THE HIGH CHURCH OF GLASGOW ON THE RASH JUDGMENT OF MAN.

GOOD old High Church, thy mould'ring pile,
    Unlike thy youthful days of yore,
Now mingles with immortal soil,
    Where thousands sleep to wake no more
Until the last loud trumpet's sound
    Shall call them from their dark abode;
From sea and land, from silent mound,
    All shall come forth to meet their God.

Thy Gothic height o'erlooks the stream
    That whispers as it murmurs by;
Alas! how little do you deem
    What countless thousands round you lie.
Sculptured marble marks the spot;
    But, ah, alas! we cannot tell
How many souls whose bodies rot,
    Shall sing in Heaven or weep in hell.

Those monuments with snowy tops,
    Erected o'er the death-like scene,
Gives unto man fictitious hopes
    That all who die in Heaven shall reign.
Some epitaphs that there we read
    Point out the soul hath fled to Heaven;
The judgment's rash—too rash indeed—
    Such judgment ne'er to man was given.

God gave to man the power to judge
    The wicked who on earth rebel;
He gave the law to lash and scourge,
    And punish in the prison cell;
But God has never given to man
    The power of judgment after death;
'Twas for himself he drew that plan,
    To judge the soul when fled the breath.

Man may remark where man is laid,
    And carve his mem'ry on the tomb,
But let it ne'er by man be said
    His soul in Heaven hath found a home—
For it is God, and God alone,
    That on the judgment-day shall tell
Who shall find in Heaven a home,
    And who for sin shall weep in hell.

Lines

TO A YOUNG GENTLEMAN OF SURPASSING BEAUTY.

HAIL! gentle youth, and do not deem me rude
    Because I dare to sing thy beauty's fame;
But I have heard that thou art kind and good,
    And freely hope you will forgive the same.

Thou canst not turn with cold contempt on me,
I am a stranger quite unknown to thee.

Pause not to ask why thou to me are known,
    While I as yet remain unknown to thee;
'Midst thy conjectures do not spurn me from
    The heaven-lit chamber of thy mem'ry;
Through thy mind's eye still gaze upon my form,
And deem me fairer than the Queen of Morn.

Ah! what am I?—A halpless child of song,
    Musing upon thy matchless beauty bright,
Tracing thy footsteps through the mazy throng,
    And gazing on thee with love-born delight.
It cheers me onward through my hopeless doom
To dream upon thy beauty's sweetest bloom.

And what art thou?—An honour'd son of wealth,
    Gay fortune's diadem sits on thy brow;
Bless'd with a generous heart, with youth and health,
    And beauty's self before thy shadow bow;
Yet thou may'st never know whose humble lays
In sadness sung thy dazzling beauty's praise.

The Marriage Morning.

Sister, arise, the sun's adorning
    The garden greenhouse o'er the way,
And nature hails thy bridal morning,
    She's dressed in robes of rich array;
The little birds are sweetly singing,
    Their songs of mirth sound o'er the plain—
Congratulations they are bringing
    To thee, my sister Mary Jane.

Ah! Mary, thou ere long will leave us—
    The best and kindest of the three;
Words cannot tell how it doth grieve us,
    Yea, even now to part with thee.
Both hope and joy together blended,
    Where doubt and fear together reign,
Although we know that thy intended
    Loves thee sincerely, Mary Jane.

When Sarah left us we felt lonely,
    When Ellen went we felt more dull,
And then when thou wert left us only
    Time made thee dearer to us still.
'Tis nature's love that fondly binds us,
    Oh what could burst her spell-bound chain
When thy generous deeds remind us
    Of thy true worth, dear Mary Jane.

No daughter left to kiss her mother
    Nor greet her father's morning smile;
No sister to salute each brother
    With fairy form and magic wile.
When mem'ry chants o'er nature's sonnet,
    When fancy brings thee back again
We'll seek thy portrait, gaze upon it,
    And bless our absent Mary Jane.

Sister, thy bridal maids await thee,
    Make haste, dear Jane, and come away;
They come for to congratulate thee
    On this thy happy marriage-day.
Yes, thou art happy, for thy bosom
    Is as free from misery's stain
As the water lily's blossom
    That wreaths thy brow, dear Mary Jane.

Sister, thy mother waits to kiss thee,
    Her soul's sincerest wish is thine;
Thy father and brothers wait to bless thee,
    And lead thee forth to Hymen's shrine.
Ah! now thou art before the altar,
    And in thy lover's love-light eyes
We read of love that ne'er can falter;
    Thy husband's worthy of his prize.

Lines
ON MISS MARGARET DORWARD SENDING HER CARTE DE VISITE AND BOUQUET OF FLOWERS TO THE AUTHORESS.

DEAR Margaret, daughter of my much loved friends,
    The 'carte de visite' thou hast sent to me
I'll keep till Death his iron hand extends,
    And leads me forth to vast eternity.
Eternity and all its endless space,
Thy form from mem'ry only can efface.

First in my album I thy 'carte' will place;
    It is the first that e'er to me was given,
No fairer form perchance its leaves may grace,
    Like a madonna gazing up to Heaven,
And musing on its holy angel band,
An earth-born angel there I see thee stand.

Thy flow'rs are wither'd—drooping in decay—
    Their leaves once beautiful in sickness fall;
Thou too must fade and mingle with the clay,
    Death is a portion that is doom'd to all.
'Tis sad to deem the beautiful must die,
But sweet to dream their souls can live on high.

May Heaven's blessing ever round thee fall,
    To thee and thine this fond wish I impart:
Long may Death linger ere he makes a call,
    To weave his chains around thy gentle heart.
May He thou lov'st above all other men,
Be true to thee and prize thee as a gem.

Lines

MOST RESPECTFULLY DEDICATED TO JAMES KENNEDY, ESQ., OF BEDFORD STREET WEAVING FACTORY, BELFAST.

AWAKE, my muse! Why dost thou sleep so long
    While honour'd worth on thee doth loudly call?
True hearts await to hear thy new-born song—
    Hearts that never felt oppression's gall,
Nor never shall while Kennedy has power
To sway commerce within fair freedom's bower.

Dear Kennedy, thy name lives in each heart
    That ever knew thy noble-hearted worth;
I heard of thee long ere I did depart
    From Scotland's shore, that dear land of my birth.
I've left her now to roam a stranger shore—
Perchance I ne'er may view her mountains more.

'Tis not alone in Erin's lovely isle
    Thy name is breath'd in gentle accents sweet,
Far, far away upon my native soil
    I've heard them speak of thee and even weep—
I heard thee bless'd, and long'd on thee to gaze,
And now I come to greet thee with my praise.

I cannot tell thy best and truest worth,
    But I will speak of what I've felt and seen.
If Erin is the land that gave thee birth,
    Proud may she be this day indeed to deem
That such a heart as thine beats in her isle—
A better master ne'er paid worker's toil.

'Tis not to thy worth in gold that I refer,
    It is thy gen'rous philanthropic love;
Thou'rt always happy when thy servants share
    Life's joys with thee, and thou dost well approve
Thy servants' worth, whatever it may be—
It makes thee glad their welfare still to see.

Thy noble brow bespeaks thy nobler mind—
    The sun of kindness beams upon thy face—
Truth and humanity we ever find
    Within thy bosom's secret dwelling place,
And veneration's snowy wings are spread
Like angel guards round thy devoted head.

Thy partner in the 'firm,' he too is all
    In face or form that woman could admire—
So graceful and so pleasant—young and tall—
    With eyes that burn like cupid's melting fire;
They pierce my bosom like a two-edged dart,
Leaving a sunshine gleaming in my heart.

The first time I beheld him gently glide
    In prince-like glee around our little shed,
I thought I would have sunk down by his side.
    He brought to mem'ry one that's long since dead—
His every look reminds me even now
Of *one* whose shadow made me humbly bow.

But youth and youthful memories are but dreams—
    Sweet while the impulse of their moments last.
Give me the man whose heart forever seems
    The solid rock we can hold firm and fast;
When tossed on fate's tempestuous raging main,
'Tis sweet 'midst death to grasp at life's gold chain.

Dear Kennedy, farewell to thee a while,
    And chide me not because I wish thee well;
Go when I may from Erin's lovely isle,
    Thy mem'ry still shall in my bosom dwell—
Remember, though a woman's weak and frail,
My prayer for thee to Heaven may avail.

The Husband's Lament.

She's gone and I am wifeless now,
    Cold death has chang'd my fate,
And sorrow clouds each youthful brow
    That shone so bright of late;
Around my hearth in gladsome mirth
They smil'd on her that gave them birth.

She's gone and left them motherless,
    Her hand with loving care
Shall never more their foreheads press,
    Nor shade their silken hair,
Nor press them fondly to her heart,
A mother's fond love to impart.

She's gone, my kind and loving wife,
    My household's guard and guide—
She who hath borne the cares of life
    With pleasure by my side,

And seemed still proud with me to share
Life's brightest joy or darkest care.

She's gone—the fatal fever's o'er—
    And all my family's well,
Save her whom tears cannot restore,
    That's gone with death to dwell;
And she is safe within that land
Where grief or care hath no command.

She's gone, and who will act the part
    Of mother to my flock?
Who will assume with hand and heart
    A mother's anxious yoke;
And soothe their childish cares to rest,
Like her that nurs'd them on her breast?

She's gone, and may the God of grace
    Place o'er my children's head
Some one that will the footsteps trace
    Of her that now lies dead;
And I will still her worth approve
Who imitates their mother's love.

The Exile of Poland.

Weep not for thy country, poor exile of Poland,
    O'er the depth of her wrongs or the gall of her chain;
But hope for the future though now she has fallen,
    That time may restore her to freedom again.

Though her laurels of honour be trampl'd and blighted,
    And her harp slumbers still in her desolate halls,
May the exiles of Poland once more be delighted
    In the homes of their fathers at banquet and ball.

But while they are here we shall never deny them
    Our dear country's best love round their hearts to enthral,
Like true philanthropists feel glad to supply them
    With the fare of our cottage or the feast of our hall.

Though the brave sons of Poland like outcasts are banished
    For to toil with the stranger who knows not their worth,
Yet we hope that oppression ere long will be vanished,
    And sweet freedom restore them the land of their birth.

Yes, we hope that the chain of oppression may sever,
    And bright sun of freedom his golden beams shower;
And the Russian eagles be fetter'd for ever,
    No longer to soar on the pinions of power.

Then gladsome as summer, in brightness careering,
    The sweet homes of their childhood shall hail them with glee
When the Russian tyrants, like clouds disappearing,
    They shall sink underneath their own dastard decree.

Weep not for thy country, poor exile of Poland!
    Ah! forbid those large tears to moisten thy cheek,
Though thy soul like a fountain of sorrow hath swollen;
    Ah! thou yet may'st rejoice in Russia's defeat.

Epitaph.

Thou art gone to thy cold and narrow bed,
    Where the worm its watch is keeping,
And the mould'ring dust now pillows thy head,
    With the death-shade o'er thee creeping;
And the deepest grief that true worth can own
Still endears thy mem'ry Catherine Thom.

Thou art gone to thy cold and narrow bed,
    And left me in sorrow sighing;
Bitter, alas! were the tears that I shed
    When I saw that thou wert dying;
And long ere life's rays were gone
I wept thy bereavement, Catherine Thom.

Thou art gone to thy cold and narrow bed,
    And I hope thou art appointed
To rest in peace with the righteous dead,
    And arise with God's annointed;
And may I meet with thee at his throne
Of life everlasting, Catherine Thom.

The Lay of a Scottish Girl.

DEAR Erin, wilt thou still thy harp?
    And I will sing to thee;
For thou hast been, sweet Emerald Queen,
    The songstress of the sea.
Thine are the bards, whose love-born muse
    Like jewell'd stars will shine,
Although they sleep in slumber deep
    Beneath their sea-girt shrine.

Dear Erin, Scotland was my home,
    The land where I was born;
Though now an exile, here I roam,
    And wander all forlorn.
Yet still I love the land wherein
    I've borne a thousand wrongs,
And spent youth's years in sighs and tears,
    Whilst others sung my songs.

And I have dwelt in foreign lands,
    Where wealth was shining bright—
And I have roamed o'er sunny strands,
    Where all seemed life and light.
I've wreath'd my brow with jessemine
    From India's balmy soil,
Yet sweeter seems the shamrock green
    Of Erin's lovely isle.

And I have danced in Italy's halls
    With lordly gallants gay,
Whose waving plumes and star-clad breasts
    Bespoke their high-born sway.
Their dazzling grandeur made me sad,
    For scorn lurked in their smile—
I prize by far, without a star,
    The youths of Erin's isle.

My native land hath heath clad hills,
    With thistles waving free;
My native land hath murmuring rills
    That wander to the sea;
But Erin hath a humble hut
    Where I may ever dwell,
Then heather hills and murmuring rills
    I bid thee now farewell.

Dear Erin, thou art now my home,
    My fate shall blend with thine;
I never more may leave thy shore,
    Let weal or woe be mine.
And when Death's hand hath laid me low,
    To slumber in thy soil,
My blessing, like a spirit bright,
    Shall beam on Erin's isle.

The Ruined Heiress.

FORGIVE thee! Never whilst life I retain;
   How canst thou dare forgiveness to entreat?
Yea, thou who didst my spotless bosom stain,
   And stung my soul with adders of deceit.

I loved thee as the sunshine loves the sea—
   As Heaven loves the holy and the just;
Thou wert my heaven—how I trusted thee?
   False-hearted villain!—thou betrayd'st my trust.

Oh give me back my purity of thought—
   The spotless love my soul did pour on thee;
With deep-dyed falsehood thou hast basely bought
   Those priceless gems of innocence from me.

Oh tear those stinging adders from my breast—
   Those clouds of shame that's branded on my brow;
Restore the peace of mind I once possess'd,
   Before I listened to thy perjur'd vow.

How could I deem thou hadst another wife,
   When thou didst kneel upon thy bended knee,
And vow'd to love me dearer than thy life,
   And called on Heaven to list—thy vow to me?

Behold the wretched wreck that thou hast left
   Of what was once a baron's joy and pride!
Of every joy on earth I am bereft—
   A wanderer, now; once thy bethrothed bride.

Behold the pride of 'Dhu!'—the favourite flower—
   Whose proud ancestors were their country's boast;
The once-loved heiress of a castle tower,
   Whose strong embattlements defend its coast.

Thou cam'st a chieftain to my father's hall,
    With angel smile thou hid'st thy demon art;
Then drained the cup of sweets, and left the gall,
    Whose dregs sent death into the old man's heart.

Perfidious villain, I would not love thee now,
    For countless worlds I would not wear thy name;
I only live to see thy perjured vow
    Consume thee with my curse lit in its flame.

Cold-hearted spoiler, from my sight depart—
    Go, weave some other victim in thy spell;
Proud, haughty lordling even as thou art,
    Thy deeds are darker than the depths of hell.

The Wrongs of Mary Queen of Scots.

When Scottish poets string their harps
    To sing of wonders new,
Of heroes brave and heroines,
    Whose numbers are but few,
I'll sing a song from history's page
    Of a darker deed once seen,
When Southern Bessie martyr'd
    Old Scotland's lovely Queen.

Thrice cursed be the cruel hand
    That drew the fatal stroke,
And severed her white neck in two
    Upon the sable block.
Her blood shall stain the Saxon's fame,
    Through centuries yet unseen,
They yet shall blush as mem'ry rush
    O'er thoughts of Scotland's Queen.

Queen Bessie said, to clear the crime,
    It was for Mary's creed
She lock'd her up in prison strong,
    Then sign'd the fatal deed;
But feeling hearts know better far,
    It was for spite and spleen;
It was not for her creed alone
    She martyr'd Scotland's Queen.

How far might Southern Bessie went
    Ere she met one so fair,
For lovely Mary Stuart was
    A matchless beauty rare;
And every man that saw her face
    Felt admiration keen,
So dazzling was the sunny smile
    Of Scotland's lovely Queen.

Oft have I dream'd I saw her glide
    By yonder castle wall,*
Dress'd in her royal war-like robes,
    Just in the twilight's fall;
And sitting on her milk white steed,
    Cross o'er from Camphill green—
A warrior, tho' a woman,
    Was Scotland's lovely Queen.

She was a flow'r of Scottish soil,
    In France adopted long,
Though England measured all her faults,
    She measured not her wrong.

---

* Haggs Castle, Pollokshaws, by Glasgow.

And many things were said of her
    That never yet was seen—
Thrice worse was she that martyred
    Old Scotland's lovely Queen.

Although I ne'er shall own her creed,
    I'll still revere her name,
And cast a sunshine o'er the shade
    That veils her royal fame.
Black though her history's pages be,
    Dark though her deeds may seem,
Yet Scotland never more may have
    A lovely Scottish Queen.

Our present Queen is just as good
    As ever Queen could be—
Long may she wear the British crown
    And rule the kingdom three.
But Scotland's might shall hold her right
    In spite of all that's been,
While Edinburgh town protects the crown
    Once worn by Scotland's Queen.

The Forsaken Maiden.

O Edward, Edward, lovely one,
    Thou hast wrapt my soul in sadness;
Why dost thine eyes, bright as the sun,
    Light my bosom unto madness?
Once my heart, in calm devotion,
    Was wrapt in love's ecstatic blaze,
Shedding beams of sweet emotion
    Through my soul's enraptured gaze.

Oh, I lov'd thee, never deeming
    Thou would'st look with scorn on me;
Now I've waken'd from my dreaming,
    Wrapt in dark clouds of misery.
Edward, I can see thee smiling
    On my rival when she's near;
I can feel thee still beguiling
    This heart of mine with love more dear.

Still thy form doth flit before me,
    Awake—asleep, still thou art near,
And my soul's love hovers o'er thee,
    Dimm'd with many a burning tear.
Thou hast left me thus forsaken,
    All lonely and dejected now,
While my heart it is a breaking,
    Pondering o'er thy broken vow.

The Baxter Statue.

CONTRIBUTION TO THE BAXTER TESTIMONIAL.
TO THE EDITOR OF THE PEOPLE'S JOURNAL.

Dear Sir,—I am poor, but to prove I am willing,
I send you my mite, though it be but a shilling;
It will aid in the movement that's now in commotion,
Of proving the people's true heartfelt devotion,
By raising a statue of honour and glory
To immortalise him in fame's golden story
That gift from dear Baxter might do a king honour—
Yet he is no king—who has been the kind donor—
No proud, haughty lordling, no prince or false prophet,
But a true feeling man—a real 'philanthropic.'

And his gentle sisters' love in their eyes beaming,
And Christian charity from their hearts teeming.
Their names like their brother's shall live on through ages,
A pattern to ladies in less varied stages.
In far away lands, amongst rich habitations,
There are linen-lords of all ranks and stations,
But it never was known of such a gift given
By a lord of commerce 'neath the blue vaults of Heaven.
No ear has yet heard it, no tongue has yet told it,
No record of history as yet has enrolled it;
With all honour due, then, let him be rewarded,
Who has honoured Dundee, and its people regarded.
O come from the mountains, the woods, and the valleys,
Come from the lanes, the wynds, and the alleys,
Come with your mite though it be but a penny,
You shall be as welcome, yea, welcome as any;
And whilst the skilled artist that statue is raising,
Our mind's eye through dreamland shall fondly be gazing
On the bright sunny future when we shall be roaming
Through the dew-spangled flowers in the good time that's
    coming.
Inhaling the breezes from river and mountain,
The sweet fragrant floweret and rock-leaping fountain,
Admiring God's great works of beautiful nature,
That tell of his wonders in each tinted feature.
That flower-woven gift, Oh what millions wear it,
And 'Old Father Time' on his iron wing shall bear it
Through centuries unseen; yea, it shall be in keeping
When he who hath given it shall be silently sleeping
Till the last trumpet's sound by God shall be given,
To call him to dwell in the mansions of Heaven.
Unborn generations shall yet wander through it,
And great men of genius with pleasure shall view it;
And his statue shall stand there to immortalise
His name like a star in the blue-vaulted skies.

Whilst the glorious Tay rolls on to the ocean,
Whilst the sun on its bosom doth beam with devotion,
As bright shall it beam on that statue of glory,
Still telling a tale of philanthropic story.
Ah! dear Baxter, the gift thou hast nobly given
Is one that shall bloom like a garden of Heaven.

The Working Man.

THE spring is come at last, my freens, cheer up, you sons of toil,
Let the seeds of independence be sown in labour's soil,
And tho' the nipping blast of care should blight your wee bit crop,
Oh dinna let your spirits sink, cling closer aye to hope.

If youth and health be on your side, you ha'e a richer boon
Than him that's dressed in royal robes and wears a diamond crown;
Nae widow's curse lies in your cup, you bear nae orphan's blame;
Nae guilty conscience haunts your dreams wi' visions of the slain·

Tho' light your purse, and worn your coat the darkest hour of night,
Is whiles the very ane that is before it dawns daylight;
And tho' your lot looks unco hard, your future prospects drear,
Hope's sun may burst through sorrow's cloud, your sinking soul to cheer

The summer's drawing near, my freens, cheer up ye sons of toil,
Let the sun of independence aye greet ye wi' a smile;
His genial beams will light your hearth when it is mirk wi' care,
When ye ha'e little for to spend, and far less for to spare.

Let him that ne'er kent labour's yoke but come to Glasgow toon,
And let him take a cannie walk her bonny buildings roon,
And let him wi' his lady hands, his cheeks sae pale and wan,
Stand face to face, without a blush, before the Working Man.

But the man who wins fair fortune wi' labour's anxious pain,
He is the man who's justly earned her favour and her fame;
And may he aye keep flourishing wherever he may gang,
And ne'er forget the days that gane when but a Working Man.

The harvest soon will be, my freens, cheer up, you sons of toil,
And the fu'some hand of plenty will store your domicile;
Ye are the sons of nature's art, aye forming some new plan,
Oh what would bonny Scotland do without the Working Man?

My Cousin Bill.

My Cousin Bill is twenty-one,
   So sprightly, young, and gay;
His dark eyes sparkle like the sun,
   His smile's like merry May.
There's melody within his voice
   That haunts my bosom still,
And makes me wish I was the choice
   Of my young 'Cousin Bill.'

Tho' I am older far than him,
   Yet always when he's near
Life seems to me a sunny dream—
   Unclouded, bright, and clear.
The sparkling glance of his dark eye,
   With magic art and skill,
Darts through my bosom—then I sigh
   For my young Cousin Bill.

I wish, indeed, that I could tell
    If this strange thing is Love—
That makes my heart so fondly swell,
    And prize him far above
All other youths that I can meet;
    For, wander where I will,
Memory clings with visions sweet
    To my young 'Cousin Bill.'

Methinks I see him near me stand,
    I hear his soft good night—
And feel the pressure of his hand—
    It fills me with delight;
But soon the dazzling phantom dies,
    The scene grows void and still;
My golden dream like vapour flies,
    And leaves no 'Cousin Bill.'

Life whirles round the wheel of time,
    Like billows o'er the sea;
But seldom meets a lot like mine—
    Oh! when shall I be free?
If fate has joy in store for me,
    May it be Heaven's will
That all those joys still shared may be
    With my sweet 'Cousin Bill.'

Perjury's Victim.

O MARY, where art thou sweetly sleeping—
    Free from the thoughts of thy false lover's vow?
Thou sleepest in peace, free from grief and weeping,
    A wreath of glory entwined round thy brow;
Gone far away from this vain wicked earth,
And leaving sorrow where thou once brought mirth.

Mary, where is he you loved sincerely,
    Who vowed you would be his and his alone?
But when the frowns of fortune came severely,
    When all thy better hopes of wealth had gone,
When thee and thine had sunk to low estate
He left thee, Mary, to thy hapless fate.

When flowing plenty cheered thy father's home,
    Each night we found him there in high toned glee;
But when the sweeping tide of fate did come,
    And left but little for thy friends and thee,
He turned with scorn and passed thy father's door—
He loved no longer, Mary—thou wert poor.

Though thou wert poor, none knew thy silent sorrow
    Unless that God who seeth from on high,
And when we gazed on thee each coming morrow,
    Thy pale thin face and dim and sunken eye,
We saw some secret grief did prey on thee,
But knew not, Mary, what the cause might be.

We little dreamed that one in Erin's isle,
    Whose heart was stained with vilest perjury,
And broken vows had won thy heart the while,
    And left the sting of grief destroying thee.
We knew not, Mary, as we know it now,
Thou wert the victim of a broken vow.

Farewell, we hope thou art a bride of Heaven,
    It matters not whom thy false love may wed,
Thou didst not wish that his hopes might be shriven,
    Nor didst invoke a curse upon his head.
Farewell, we leave thee slumb'ring in the dust,
God will avenge thy wrongs, for He is just.

Lines

ON BEHALF OF THE BOATBUILDERS AND BOILERMAKERS OF GREAT BRITAIN AND IRELAND.

O THAT I could rob fortune of her gold as she has robbed the poor man of his rights, I would give each worthy man his share, and then would thousands live who die for want of that which some of those who are less worthy have too much.—*The Factory Girl.*

SHALL England's rose no longer bloom
　　In freedom's sunny bower?
Must her brave sons drop in the tomb
　　Of aristocratic power?

Shall Ireland's lovely shamrock green
　　No longer from her soil
Spring forth to greet young beauty's queen,
　　And honour Erin's isle.

Shall Scotland's thistle be no more
　　The glory of her land?
The song of Scottish freedom's lore
　　The soul of patriot's band?

*　　*　　*　　*　　*　　*　　*

O gather hay while the sun shines
　　All ye who wish to be free;
Nip, ere too late, the chain that binds
　　The gems of sweet liberty.

Why will ye hesitate longer
　　While cruel despotic power
Is working the chain still stronger
　　That draws on the evil hour?

Our brothers in prison were cast*
    Because like brave men they spoke,
When crushed in the powerful grasp
    Of slavery's galling yoke.

Shall our democrats still be slaves—
    Still unknown to fortune's smile—
And drop into premature graves
    The victims of ill paid toil?

Shall their children cry out for bread,
    And mothers have none to give,
And die—but ere they are dead
    Curse the hour that saw them live?

Shall tyrants exalt o'er the spoil
    Of gold that was ne'er their own—
Gold obtained by the poor man's toil,
    Which to his children belong?

Shall a Britain e'er yield a stroke
    To build up a noble bark?
Then turn him round and scorn the spot,
    And say with a haughty heart—

That he will not support the cause
    Which upholds his country's right,
But still sustain the unjust laws
    Of aristocratic might.

Shall the rich man behold his ship
    With her gallant mast and bow,
Moistened with sweat on the slip,
    Wrung out from the poor man's brow?

* Referring to the tin-plate workers of England.

And still deny to him the wage
    That he has so justly earned,
With his care-worn face stamped with age
    Ere his youth was well discerned.

Ye rich! who hath gained fortune's heart,
    How greedy your selfish souls;
Thou the poor man ne'er spares a part
    Of pleasure which round ye rolls.

Yet still ye would trample him down;
    Yes, down to sixpence a day,
For work that is well worth a pound,
    Were justice dealt in his pay.

The money ye hoard in your purse
    Like the treasures of your soul,
And it crieth out with a curse,
    Because of the 'launching bowl.'

Which gave to each man joy and mirth
    The night when his well-finished work
Was launched from the place of its birth,
    To brave both sea and shark.

But now ye'll not spare him a groat
    That he might drink your good health,
And wish speed to the gallant boat,
    To return again with wealth.

Woe! on the deep-dyed crimson shame
    Of those that would e'er do so,
And tinge their might-betitled name
    With actions so mean and low.

Though the poor man shares no great fame,
    Save a toil-worn soul nigh riven;
Still, with the rich man he can claim
    Both rest and peace in Heaven.

All ye who toil by the river,
   Now is the day and the hour.
Be your watchword—'Union for ever,'
   Till union has gold in its power.

So gather ye hay while the sun shines,
   The union's harvest secure;
Reap well while yet there's no fierce winds,
   'Prevention is better than cure.'

Lines

TO MR JAMES DORWARD, POWER-LOOM FOREMAN, CHAPELSHADE WORKS, DUNDEE,

THE FIRST AND BEST FRIEND TO THE AUTHORESS IN THE DEEPEST HOURS OF HER TRIALS AND TRIBULATIONS IN DUNDEE.

THE summer's come again, Jamie, twa happy years ha'e fled
Since ye gied me a limm, Jamie, in the dear Chapelshade;
And I will ne'er forget that time until the day I dee,
That happy blessed morning when ye gied that limm to me.

O I was sorry then, Jamie, a wand'ring poor exile,
Begging my brothers of the earth to gie me leave to toil;
Pale poverty stood at my door, my hope on earth was fled,
Until I found a resting-place within the Chapelshade.

There was muckle said and dune, Jamie, by mair than ane or twa,
To take frae me my limm, Jamie, and get me turned awa;
But ye were my faithful friend in need, and I will ne'er forget,
Until I'm numbered wi' the dead, how deep I'm in your debt.

And may Heaven bless ye, Jamie, and a' your kith and kin,
For ye ha'e left it in my power the victory for to win;
I've conquered a' my foes, Jamie, that did my ruin plan,
And noo I bid defiance to every perjured man.

While you are on my side, Jamie, I carena a bawbee
For a' the West-end tenters that ever screwed a key;
I'm happy as a queen, Jamie, in the bonny Chapelshade,
And whilst you're pleased to keep me there, wi' you I'll earn
    my bread.

And wha are they would blame, Jamie, altho' I wish ye weel?
For words can never name, Jamie, the gratitude I feel;
Ye are the first, the truest friend I've met wi' in Dundee,
And whate'er may be my future lot, I'll bless your mem'ry.

May Heaven bless your wife, Jamie, wha aye will share a part
Of the never dying gratitude that lives within my heart;
May God restore her better health, and may she live to see
Her bairns' bairns smiling in manhood's pride and glee.

And may your bonny Maggie be as gude as she is fair,
Likewise your absent Ellen, that's beneath anither's care;
May their lot through life be happy, and God still be their guide—
May they be their father's comfort, their mother's joy and pride.

And may William, George, and Thomas, all grow up useful men,
Ah! gie them lots o' learning—make them masters o' the pen;
The man that's master o' the pen is master o' an art,
That on the tower o' science still hauds the master part.

And may your dear Elizabeth, and Agnes your wee pet,
And your wee rosebud, Davy, ne'er cause ye to regret;
But twine like ivy round your heart wi' love that still endears,
And licht like sunshine in a storm the winter o' your years.

Frae the bottom o' my heart, Jamie, thus I wish for thee—
May you and yours aye be as weel as I wish ye would be;
May health and wealth and joy and love aye round your hearth
    be spread;
Long may ye be my foreman in the bonny Chapelshade.

Your Wee Neebour Nell.

A GUDE happy New-Year tae ye, Mrs Moncrieff,
May ye ne'er feel the saut tears o' sorrow nor grief,
Nor adversity's winds that are baith keen an' snell—
Oh! that is the heart's wish o' your wee neebour Nell.

I ne'er will forget when ye warned me o' strife
That was brewing unseen for tae canker my life,
And sae couthy an' kindly ye did tae me tell—
Oh! the false friends betraying your wee neebour Nell.

And I ne'er will forget o' the days when near dead,
When my e'en wad grow blin wi' the pain o' my head,
Ye wad bid me cheer up, and strange stories ye'd tell,
A' tae wear in the day wi' your wee neebour Nell.

And whiles in the mornings when drenched to the skin,
When my boots they were wet ye wad gae me your shune,
Ye wad stuff them wi' tow, and wad want them yersel',
And jist a' tae oblige your puir wee neebour Nell.

Your sweet wee Eliza, who sleeps noo in the yaird,
Oh! how peaceful her slumber, the bonny wee bird;
And she kens nae the story her mither could tell
O' the days that are gane tae her wee neebour Nell.

Oh! I am wearying sair for the spring o' the year
For tae bring back your Jamie ye've lang lo'ed so dear;
It is ten years and mair since he bade ye farewell,
But ye'll meet him again wi' your wee neebour Nell.

And may ye live happy a' the rest o' your life;
May he be a true husband as ye've been a wife;
And in peace, love, and comfort oh! may ye aye dwell,
And see mony New-Years wi' your wee neebour Nell.

Lines to a Sick Friend.

O that I could a balsam find
    To ease thy burning smart;
Believe, dear friend, I have the mind—
    Nay, more, I have the heart.

And though that heart it may be pledged
    To one that's far away,
With faithful friendship it's engaged
    To whom—I will not say.

No, my dear friend, I'll breathe no name,
    But leave thee this to guess,
Lest it might bring a blush of shame
    Would I the truth confess.

But if you come to Dundee fair
    I'll whisper in thine ear
A secret that I would not care
    Though all the world would hear.

One friendly kiss I now enclose,
    That kiss it is for thee;
I've placed it on this little rose,
    Its impress you shall see.

Oh press it to those lips of thine,
    A charm it may impart,
For thy dear name like ivy twine
    Around my grateful heart.

And in some corresponding breeze,
    Ah! waft one back to me;
I'll prize it, and on bended knees
    I'll breathe a prayer for thee.

Farewell until we meet again,
    May Heaven thy guardian be;
Ah! if my love could ease thy pain,
    To-day thou would'st be free!

The Drygate Brae, or Wee Mary's First Love.

O JOHNNIE, do ye mind o' the happy days o' langsyne,
    Before my mither cam' to Dundee,
When thegether we did play alang the Drygate Brae,
    Whaur you first stole my wee heart frae me.

O Johnnie, weel you ken that we were happy then,
    Thegether han' and han' we wad stray,
Wi' Maggie by our side in gladsome joy and pride
    We rambled ower the Drygate Brae.

We rowed upon the green, and your twa bonny e'en,
    Far blacker than the ripe glossy slae,
Sent young Cupid's dart through my puir wee lassie-heart,
    And I lost it on the Drygate Brae.

But years since syne ha'e fled, an' numbered wi' the dead;
    My auld grannie lies cauld in the clay;
An' here in sweet Dundee, whaur nae freens I can see,
    I am wandering frae the Drygate Brae.

Though noo we're torn apart, believe me my young heart
    A keeping in your bosom you ha'e;
Forever you shall prove my first and only love,
    Though I'm far noo frae the Drygate Brae.

I never may return to the wee hoose by the burn,
    Whaur we aft spent the lang summer's day;
Yet, Johnnie, aye you'll be my first love dear to me,
    Though I'm far noo frae the Drygate Brae.

An Address to Kelvin Water.

Flow on, lovely Kelvin! thy rock-leaping fountain
   My memory hath bound with a mystical spell,
As often I wandered thy beauties recounting,
   And drank the cool spring of thy famed three-tree-well:

Or climbed like a wild fawn thy broom-bosomed wildwood,
   That reared its green towers o'er thy blaeberry fell;
Thou heaven-like scenes of my innocent childhood—
   Ah! who would not wish with thee ever to dwell.

How often my tiny feet have I devested
   Of their stockings and shoes, when I've hither been led
By the hand of some playmate, where we unmolested,
   Would gather the peebles from their pure watery bed.

And laughed at the tiny fish while it was sporting
   At its hide-an'-go-seek round its water-cave home,
While the poor silly fly thy bright mirror courting
   Would drop to caress thee, and find thee its tomb;

And the old wooden bridge o'er thy bosom extended,
   It would quake like an aspen beneath our light forms.
For its old rotten wood-beams were broken and bended;
   They for ages had stood many rude winter storms.

The little white house at the end of its landing
   Was curtained with foliage from tall stately trees
That bowed to and fro like spirits demanding
   A kiss for a sigh from the sweet balmy breeze.

The milky white hawthorn and sweet honeysuckle
   That walled thy green margin with gowans arrayed;
And the bright golden buttercup twined round the thistle,
   The blue-bell and primrose their beauties displayed.

And the little farm-house farther eastward thy winding,
    With its foreground or garden with flowers richly spread;
Ah! where is it now?—alas! there is no finding
    The dear spot where once stood the cosey homestead.

The snowy-white swans in its little lake swimming,
    And the old parent hen watching o'er her young brood;
The proud flaunting peacock majestically screaming—
    'Midst his feathery tribe, there a monarch he stood.

The large curly mastiff would cease his loud baying,
    And would crouch back again to his straw-couched abode;
And the peacock, as if he thought us surveying
    The gorgeous gems of his bright spangled robe,

Would spread his gay wings that like diamonds would glitter,
    While the sun his bright radiance downwards would fling;
Then his feathery flock would all join in a chatter,
    As if they sung praise to their beautiful king.

The tortoiseshell cat on her sentry parading,
    And still scanning her prey with wild looks of alarm;
The unconscious sparrows freely pervading
    The holes in the wall, never dreaming of harm.

Then the good wife, perchance, would wonder what ailed us,
    And then gaze in our face with such motherly care;
Then ask us so kindly if hunger assailed us—
    Ay, ye canna miss, weans, ye've been lang waiting there.

Then would reach us a bowl, with milk overflowing,
    And a large oaten bannock, with butter well spread;
With smiles in her face that bespoke a heart glowing,
    With love like to hers who sleeps now with the dead.*

        * My mother.

But young hearts like to ours but rarely felt hunger,
    We would feast on thy beauty and drink of thy well,
Till the gold veil of twilight around us would linger,
    And Luna's dark curtain in sable folds fell.

Where now are those playmates? Ah! some sweetly sleeping;
    In the North Street church-yard they now mingle with dust;
And some far in Australia for dame fortune seeking—
    Some are struggling like me here to earn their life's crust.

And our old Father Time as onward he hurries,
    Young and old, rich and poor must brook to his sway;
On his iron-bound back our fortune he carries,
    While fate weaves our lot, be that lot what it may.

Ah! mine was a hard one, with thorns ever springing,
    Intercepting my footsteps where'er I would stray,
And each coming morrow a new sorrow bringing,
    Bright hopes born and buried often times in one day.

Now gay lovers and friends around me are teeming,
    When the bloom of my youth is beginning to wane;
In the fall of my life's leaves hope's bright sun is gleaming,
    And the days of my youth seems returning again.

Oh, Kelvin! sweet Kelvin! immortal in story,
    Where beauty and grandeur supremely doth reign;
Thou fountain of love's fame and river of glory,
    Ere long I may wander o'er thy green banks again.

The Factory Girl's Farewell.

FAREWELL to Galbraith's bonnie mill,
    Where long I've earned my daily bread;
Where many a shuttle I did fill,
    With bursting heart and aching head.

The griefs that I have undergone,
    Language hath no power to tell;
But God shall yet repay each wrong,
    So Galbraith's bonnie mill, farewell!

It was not thee, nor was it those
    Who toil in thee that caused my grief;
Dark Envy wrecked my calm repose,
    And long I sighed to find relief.
Ah! mine were deep-dyed, countless wrongs,
    Which did from Falsehood's bosom swell;
I've wept whilst others sung my songs,
    So Galbraith's bonnie mill, farewell!

I go not hence in grief nor shame,
    Within a stranger-land to range;
I go to wear another's name—
    My heart for his give in exchange.
And he hath pledged when I'm his wife,
    Care's dark clouds he will dispel;
And prize me as a gem through life,
    So Galbraith's bonnie mill, farewell!

I go to live in London town,
    Amidst the wealthy and the fair;
I may not reach to high renown;
    But if I have contentment there,
That is the love-born star of mirth,
    It hath a conquering power to quell
The pangs which sorrow giveth birth:
    So Galbraith's bonnie mill, farewell!

Farewell to one, farewell to all,
    And those who were my truest friends;
Their memory shall my heart enthrall,
    When other hearts their love extends.

Farewell to James and Thomas Locke,
    And Robert Rankin I'll wish well,
Until Death draws his fatal stroke:
    So Galbraith's bonnie mill, farewell.

Farewell, John Fairlie and James Weir,
    'Dick,' 'Tom,' and 'Jim,' and number *One*,
The Brothers Lambert, not long here,
    And likewise Samuel Sunderland,
Whose sunny smile and swelling song
    Oft bound me in a mystic spell,
And soothed me with its melting tone:
    So Galbraith's bonnie mill, farewell!

Farewell to all the works around,
    The flax mill, foundry, cooperage too;
The old forge, with its blazing mound,
    And Tennant's stalk, farewell to you.
Your gen'rous masters were so kind,
    Theirs was the gift that did excel;
Their name around my heart is twined:
    So Galbraith's bonnie mill, farewell!

Farewell, my honour'd masters two,
    Your mill no more I may traverse;
I breathe you both a fond adieu;
    Long may you live lords of commerce.
Farewell unto my native land,
    Land of the thistle and blue-bell;
Oh! wish me joy with heart and hand:
    So Galbraith's bonnie mill, farewell!

The Lost Purse.

Oh, fare-thee-well, my lovely purse,
    Thy glittering clasp I'll ne'er see more;
Thy envious thief I will not curse,
    Who stole thee to enrich her store—
Not for ten thousand times thy gain
Would I wear thy thief's vile stain.

'Tis true thy loss brought grief to me;
    And, though I have not much to spare,
I rather would the loser be
    Than she who heartlessly did bear
Thee from my cupboard, where you lay,
With thy contents her debt to pay.

'Twas not thy loss alone brought grief,
    'Twas disappointment yea to find
A trusted friend turn out a thief;
    The thought would ne'er have crossed my mind
That such a friend would turn a foe,
And add so deeply to my woe.

She saw me struggling, day by day,
    With feeble heart and aching head,
And yet she stole my purse away,
    And left me nought to buy my bread;
Yet told me at the very time
A better lot it should be mine.

Just four half-crowns in silver cash,
    And four halfpence was all thy claim.
Who stole my purse did steal but trash;
    But if she spare my crown of fame,
I'll leave her to enrich herself—
Yes, with my hard-won scanty wealth.

Although to me thou'rt ever lost,
    A pleasant joy it doth impart—
That o'er the world I can boast
    An honoured name, an honest heart.
Not for the wealth of England's throne
Would I take what is not my own.

Farewell, my purse, a last adieu;
    May God thy heartless thief forgive;
The grief I've found in losing you
    Shall make me careful while I live.
No more thy loss I will repine,
For God hath said 'Vengeance is mine.'

Address

TO THE FACTORY OF MESSRS. J. & W. I. SCOTT & CO.,

JOHN STREET, BRIDGETON.

HAIL! Royal Sovereign of the Factory race,
    Thrice do I hail thee on thy gorgeous throne;
And in thy queen-like lineaments I trace
    Thy worth as matchless as it is unknown.
How vast are thy dominions and thy wealth?
Thou hold'st a city's commerce by thyself.

The faithful porter at thy monarch gate,
    Through thy long arch doth cast his watchful eyes,
No stragglers see thee in thy queen-like state,
    Nor see thy royal structures round thee rise;
Nor enter thy back shed, so large and grand,
The boast of Scotland's manufacturing land.

Thy cotton palace from my left doth stand,
    A gem that England's cotton lords might prize;
Thy counting-house is placed at my right hand,
    Where will ye find its match, 'tis such a size?
And o'er thy snowy walls of massive pile
The king of commerce seems to sit and smile.

And when I cross thy wide expanding court,
    Hundreds of thy daughters I meet there;
Their young eyes lighted up with gladsome sport,
    Their handsome forms and faces, sweet and fair.
O! lovely Sovereign! thou dost bear the fame
Of daughters fair that wear a fairer name.

Thy sons, too, are the bravest of the brave,
    Their fame is spread throughout the Scottish land;
Love, truth, and honour, o'er their head doth wave,
    And duty sways them both in heart and hand:
And thy cross-over-looms can truly tell,
Few with their skilful genius can excel.

Give to thy stockers every honour due,
    Thy pickers, carders, spinners, act their part;
Thy engineers, and thy mechanics, too,
    Are all sufficient in mechanic art.
Thy tapers, twisters, tenters, well may boast
Of many honours other men have lost.

Thy clerks, too, are a class of active men,
    So civil and polite in every form;
With unassuming grace they use their pen,
    Their faces free from cold contemptuous scorn,
And all thy managers, they are the same—
True to their trust—what more could duty claim?

But listen yet, I have a tale to tell,
    It is of younger years, when life was sweet,
Long ere you came into this land to dwell,
    I lived a happy child in Muslin Street;
And where thou standest now, I've gathered flowers,
And spent my sweetest, purest—childhood hours.

Near Edward's church, there stood an old grey wall,
    And further on a long green avenue—
O'er one side, many a clustering branch did fall,
    And on the other, a lovely hawthorn grew;
Oh! God, could memory die, and hide from sight
Those early scenes that haunt me day and night.

Old Father Time hath changed the scenes since then,
    And who shall call the tale I tell untrue;
Thy gorgeous arch that now inspires my pen,
    Stands on the spot where stood that avenue,
And where I sat in childhood's sunny smile,
I stand each day now at my daily toil.

And I am also changed—Fate's hand hath passed,
    And branded dark misfortunes on my brow;
O'er my young heart she breathed her withering blast,
    And like the leaves that fall from autumn's bough,
She scattered my young hopes unto the wind,
And left me here a leafless stem behind.

But, like a child, I'll cling unto thy breast,
    For there the milk of human kindness flows;
And whilst thou wear the crown—'tis my request,
    That thou thy philanthropic love will show,
And let me ever kneel before thy shrine,
Rejoicing still—prosperity is thine.

The Last Sark.

WRITTEN IN 1859.

Gude guide me, are you hame again, an' ha'e ye got nae wark,
We've naething noo tae put awa' unless yer auld blue sark;
My head is rinnin' roon about far lichter than a flee—
What care some gentry if they're weel though a' the puir
    wad dee!

Our merchants an' mill masters they wad never want a meal,
Though a' the banks in Scotland wad for a twelvemonth fail;
For some o' them have far mair goud than ony ane can see—
What care some gentry if they're weel though a' the puir
    wad dee!

This is a funny warld, John, for it's no divided fair,
And whiles I think some o' the rich have got the puir folk's
    share,
Tae see us starving here the nicht wi' no ae bless'd bawbee—
What care some gentry if they're weel though a' the puir
    wad dee!

Oor hoose ance bean an' cosey, John; oor beds ance snug an
    warm
Feels unco cauld an' dismal noo, an' empty as a barn;
The weans sit greeting in oor face, and we ha'e noucht to gie—
What care some gentry if they're weel though a' the puir
    wad dee!

It is the puir man's hard-won toil that fills the rich man's
    purse;
I'm sure his gouden coffers they are het wi' mony a curse;
Were it no for the working men what wad the rich men be?
What care some gentry if they're weel though a' the puir
    wad dee!

My head is licht, my heart is weak, my een are growing
    blin';
The bairn is faen' aff my knee—oh! John, catch haud o' him,
You ken I hinna tasted meat for days far mair than three;
Were it no for my helpless bairns I wadna care to dee.

Lines
MOST RESPECTFULLY DEDICATED TO MR JAMES DORWARD.*

DEAR CHAPELSHADE FACTORY! once more I hail thee,
    For one of thy brave sons doth claim honour's lays;
Whate'er be the fate that in future assail me,
    This night I will sing thee a song in his praise.

For worthy is he of our hearts' deep devotion,
    And worthy is he of our souls' grateful love;
The kindness he has shown us with heartfelt emotion,
    Cold death from our bosoms can only remove.

Believe us, James Dorward, we ne'er can forget thee—
    Thy kindness to us in the dear Chapelshade;
And here in the Thistle Hall this night we've met thee,
    Now our hearts' grateful thanks before thee we spread.

Thy skill as a foreman has gained admiration,
    Thou hast aimed at our welfare in each daily plan;
O long may you fill that same situation,
    We never would wish for a better foreman.

* This poem was written on the memorable occasion of Mr James Dorward being presented with a handsome sofa, as a token of gratitude and respect, from the workers under his charge in the power loom department of Chapelshade Works, on the 7th February, 1866, in the Thistle Hall, Union Street, Dundee.

For thine is the power that justice governeth—
　Thou art partial to none and pleasant to all
That in our dear factory their daily bread earneth—
　Sweet spot of freedom where no tyrants enthral.

Then take from its workers this spontaneous token,
　Perhaps those that's met here may ne'er meet again;
Though the love that they feel can never be spoken,
　On memory its impress shall ever remain.

When thy work in the factory thou hast attended,
　And the shadows of evening around thee entwine;
When thy daily labour is duly suspended,
　At home on this 'sofa' then shalt thou recline.

When dear household treasures around thee are singing
　Their sweet infant prattles of love pure and true;
When bright dreams of pleasure around thee are clinging,
　May peace be thy waking and joy greet thy view.

Then take it, James Dorward, with good-will 'tis given,
　Had it cost us ten thousand 'twould be welcome to thee;
Take with it our blessing, which is, that kind Heaven
　May guard thee and thine where'er you may be.

The Opening of the Baxter Park.

The ninth day of September
The sun arose in splendour,
His glory to surrender
　To Sir David of Dundee.
The Trades came forth in grandeur,
Each led by its commander,
Bold as an Alexander
　Of eighteen sixty-three.

Rosettes and ribbons flowing,
A radiant hue bestowing
On bosoms warmly glowing,
   Where freedom's fire ran through;
Their banners gaily swelling
Hailed from each hall and dwelling,
Their mottoes proudly telling,
   'Give honour where it's due.'

They, with their drums a-beating,
The Barrack Park did meet in,
Hailed with a hearty greeting,
   Saluted with three cheers;
With eyes like star-lights dancing
With drawn swords brightly glancing,
So warlike and entrancing
   Were our brave Volunteers.

God bless our gallant sailors,
Our shoemakers and tailors,
Our engineers and nailers,
   With all their kith and kin!
May our gardeners gather honey,
Our bakers still have money,
Our autumn still be sunny
   Till our crops are gathered in.

Our Queen, peace rest upon her!
Her Noble Lord of honour
Came here to greet the Donor
   Of *our* Park, and got the key
To open for our pleasure
That lovely flower-gemmed treasure,
Where we may sport at leisure,
   When from our toil set free.

May the brightest boon of Heaven
To the Baxter race be given!
When from us they are riven
    Their loss we will deplore.
The statue of their glory,
Immortalised in story,
Shall stand through ages hoary,
    Till time shall be no more.

Lines
IN MEMORY OF MARY WATSON PARKER.

'Suffer little children to come unto me, and forbid them not: for of such is the kingdom of God.'—LUKE XVIII., v. 16.

FAREWELL, sweet Child, our dearest household treasure;
    Young star of hope, that shone around our hearth,
Swelling our souls with love-born joy and pleasure—
    Pleasure too pure for this vain sinful earth.

We nursed thee, earth-born gem, and angel beauty;
    We gave thee constant care by night and day,
Ours, the vigilant watch, the faithful duty,
    Till Death the Spoiler, in his dark array,

Stole like a thief into thine infant bosom,
    Blighting the smile upon thy coral lip,
When like the rosebud ripening into blossom,
    His withering breath thy youthful bloom did nip.

We saw thee change, thine eyes grow dim with sickness,
    The music of thine angel voice was hushed;
We heard thee sighing only in thy weakness—
    Death's iron hand thy little heart had crushed.

One quivering smile, his fatal stroke was given;
    He left that smile still ling'ring on thy face,
Thy little soul had winged its flight to Heaven
    To dwell with Jesus round His throne of Grace.

In vain we called upon our God to save thee;
    In vain we wept around thy cradle bed;
We strove to bind thee, but the God that gave thee
    Called thee to slumber with the righteous dead.

In silent sadness now we do remove thee,
    Where sin and sorrow have no powerful sway;
Still our fond hearts can never cease to love thee,
    Although we leave thee slumbering in the clay.

Sweet offspring of our son, we loved thee dearer,
    Yes, dearer far than hadst thou been our own;
Thy Mother's death did bind thee still more nearer,
    The love we had for thee it was unknown.

Thy Mother was unto our son united,
    A happier pair ne'er dwelt upon this earth;
Ten golden moons their marriage bed had lighted
    When they in gladness smiled upon thy birth.

That morn we saw thee in her bosom lying,
    She smiled on thee—a mother and a wife;
In twelve days hence we saw thy mother dying—
    She purchased death by bringing thee to life.

We brought thee home in hopes thou would'st be cherished,
    An emblem of that dear departed one;
But now with thee our earthly hopes have perished,
    Thy father's wifeless, childless, and alone.

How soon our earthly joys can melt to sorrow,
    How soon our golden dreams can pass away;
We live to-night, but ere it dawns to-morrow
    We may be stretched a lifeless mould of clay.

Galbraith's Trip.*

AWAKE, my muse, why dost thou slumber still,
    While honour'd worth on thee doth loudly call;
Arise, and sing a song to Galbraith's mill,
    And let thy gratitude each heart enthral:
For while its master doth Lord Provost sit,
Its workers shall remember Galbraith's trip.

A happier trip, I'm sure, has never been,
    Since first King Commerce sway'd his golden reed,
And genius first invented power by steam,
    To make the shuttle fly with lightning speed;
Since weft was spun in frames, on wheels to slip,
Unparalleled is Galbraith's pleasure trip.

When golden autumn smiled upon her store,
    And swallows sought oblivion's dark abode;
When barns were filled till they could hold no more,
    And granaries sighed beneath their harvest load;
When bramble berries hung in clustering jet—
Such was the time we chose for Galbraith's Trip.

---

* These lines were written on a late pleasure excursion of the workers employed in Messrs A. & A. Galbraith's Spinning and Weaving Mills, Garngad Road, St Rollox, Glasgow.

The 10th day of September dawned with rain—
    A gloomy cloud was mantled o'er the sky;
The rising sunbeams, tinged with crimson stain,
    Foretelling mid-day would be fair and dry;
One cried by one we'll have a good day yet;
Hurrah! my lads, cheer up for Galbraith's Trip.

We joined the Cardiff Castle at the quay,
    Waving our banners of White, Red, and Blue,
Old England's glorious flag of liberty;
    To win the day the conquering sword she drew,
Deep in the foeman's heart its blade to dip—
She gained the victory, and we gained a trip.

Our men had all rosettes upon their breasts—
    Some White, Red, and Blue, some Blue and White—
Those colours shall on Britain's bosom rest,
    Though nation still with nation fiercely fight;
No foreign foe our kingdom's right shall strip,
While men survive like those at Galbraith's Trip.

Clutha never hailed with genial smile
    A worthier party than she did that day;
Our honour'd Provost's humble sons of toil,
    Linked hand and heart in union's social sway;
Proud might his Lordship be with Lords to sit,
And see his workers turn out such a trip.

The signal given, away the Cardiff flew,
    An ocean sprite, full of life and pride;
Six hundred living souls besides her crew,
    And band, whose music charmed the winding Clyde;
Queen Harmony upon the bow did sit,
Wearing the Crown we had at Galbraith's Trip.

Joy and contentment beamed on every face,
    With singing, dancing, music everywhere;
No matter where we went, we still could trace
    The sweet endearments of enjoyment there;
No gloomy care, with chilling breath, did nip
The hearts of those that were at Galbraith's Trip.

On golden wings the hours flew swift away,
    (Sweet hours, we wish thee back, but all in vain);
And as we sailed o'er Rothesay's lovely bay,
    It seemed as old heads wore young hearts again;
Old women crying, 'Ae, ma sides will split,
I ne'er saw siccan fun as Galbraith's Trip.'

In Rothesay town we found a spacious hall,
    And there we did refresh our social throng,
And then one of our Committee did call
    Some of our girls up to sing a·song,
And two did sing—but prudence will permit
To leave their names unknown at Galbraith's Trip.

And as the glass went round with mirth and glee,
    We pledged our honour'd masters' life and health,
With grateful hearts we gave them three times three,
    For we enjoyed the blessing of their wealth;
For they to us a handsome sum did slip,
To get refreshments at our pleasure trip.

Much honour's due unto our Committee—
    An active part has been performed by them;
I've been at many a trip, but ne'er did see
    So many active and ingenious men;
They will bring credit wheresoe'er they sit,
Those who conducted Galbraith's Pleasure Trip.

We landed safe, and now our trip is o'er,
 And we have all resumed our work again,
And may our labour flourish on the shore,
 Jewelled with records of our masters' fame;
Tho' time around their brows her wreaths doth knit,
Long may they live to see their workers' Trip.

Tennants' Excursion.
MOST RESPECTFULLY DEDICATED TO THE WORKMEN BY E. J. THE FACTORY GIRL.*

I've mused on pleasure trips and titled men;
 Their names I have immortalised in fame;
Their cold ingratitude disgrac'd my pen,
 And made me deem I ne'er would muse again;
I'll sing to-night of men that far outstrip
 Some lords recorded in a pleasure trip.

Hail! lordly masters of yon towering stalk,
 Whose mystic breath blends with the bright blue sky;
Around whose cavern mouth the grey clouds walk,
 Kissing its lips of dark and inky dye;
Upon whose tower the King of Commerce sits,
 Wishing success to Tennants' pleasure trip.

The rippling stream rolls onward through the bridge,
 Where countless forms are moving to and fro,
And smiling traffic floats upon its surge—
 Wave follows wave, but whence no man can know;
The hazy dawn, with rising sunbeams lit,
 Are hailing the hour for Tennants' pleasure trip.

* These verses were written on a late pleasure excursion of those employed in Charles Tennant & Co.'s, St Rollox, Glasgow, on Saturday, 22nd September, 1860.

The Queen of Autumn smiles upon the scene;
    The hand of day hath drawn her veil aside;
The vaults of Heaven distilling showers of rain
    Hath cast a gloom o'er cherished hopes of pride;
With love-lit eyes and joy upon each lip,
    Still they are bounding on to Tennants' trip.

Gather, gather, ye scientific men,
    All ye who daily toil in secret art;
Your genius is worthy to inspire the pen
    Of many a nobler true poetic heart
Than mine; for now I feel I'm scarcely fit
    To tell the beauties of Tennants' pleasure trip.

See their banners waving in the breeze,
    The glorious emblem of departed yore;
The flag of Liberty that braved the seas
    In battle for a thousand years or more,
And shall in glory brave a thousand yet—
    They have brave Volunteers at Tennants' trip.

They have three noble steeds bedeck'd with flowers,
    Woven in garlands o'er and o'er their back;
Their lofty heads are waving like the towers
    Of fairy lands which we in fancy track;
Honour'd are they whose lot it is to sit
    Upon those princely steeds at Tennants' trip.

They have three bands with instruments of brass,
    Swelling their music on the morning air,
Rousing the gods that slumber in Parnass,
    Amidst unfading Muses ever fair;
The God of Genius his gold curtains slip
    Aside to gaze on Tennants' pleasure trip.

Here comes a flute band with its thrilling notes,
    Its cadence falls upon our listening ear;
That soft strange music that so often floats
    On evening hours beneath the moonbeams clear;
Sweet are the strains that swell on rosy lip
    Of youthful swains at Tennants' pleasure trip.

Onward, ye sons of toil, linked hand and heart,
    Three gorgeous steamers await you at the quay;
And since the days of Noah's mighty ark,
    A nobler trip did never sail the sea;
There's men of every trade in Union knit,
    Firm as a rock, at Tennants' pleasure trip.

St Rollox bands are not yet in their prime,
    And of their music we can scarcely boast;
But *this* we dare to say: just give them time,
    And they ere long will gain the highest toast;
Their present rivals they will far outstrip,
    And be the gem of Tennants' coming trip.

See they are safe on Colintrave shore,
    And now the glory of the day begins;
Now the workmen chooseth half a score
    To try a race, and he that first shall win,
A silver crown unto himself they'll slip,
    To spend the day at Tennants' pleasure trip.

Now they are rambling o'er the hills of heath,
    Some pulling rowans, others the heather bell,
Some climbing nut-trees till they are out of breath,
    And startling the wild fox from its cozey cell;
Some gathering wild slaes, waving black as jet;
    They are all busy at Tennants' pleasure trip.

The blacksmith's anvil it is now forsook,
　　The plumber has forgot his leaden pipe,
The cooper's thrown aside his iron hoop,
　　The joiner's plane is hidden out of sight,
The mason's mell is resting on his kit—
　　He's hewing heather down at Tennants' trip.

The moulder's casting lies within the sand,
　　The pattern of the skilful engineer
With care is placed aside by his own hand,
　　The slater's ladder rests upon its bier,
The bricklayer's trowel in the lime doth stick—
　　He's building towers of fun at Tennants' trip.

The labouring man forgets the toil and care
　　That ofttimes spring like thorns around his hearth,
Upon his brow we trace no sorrow there;
　　His merry laugh bespeaks his heartfelt mirth,
His rosy children o'er the heath hills skip,
　　He is a king at Tennants' pleasure trip.

Duncan's brass band claims much honour due,
　　It is well known they played a noble part;
Soul-stirring was the music which they blew,
　　Casting a sunshine o'er each joyous heart,
Chasing away the shadow of regret,
　　The 'Picket Standard' at Tennants' pleasure trip.

Sons of St Rollox! welcome home again,
　　The day in matchless pleasure ye have passed;
Oh, that such pleasure with you would remain,
　　Such earthly joys are far too bright to last;
This day is gone, leaving no sad regret,
　　Its like shall come again at Tennant's trip.

Ye men who wear dear Erin's shamrock green,
　　Within your hearts the guide-star of your life;
Ye sons of Scotland's thistle, sharp and keen,
　　Whose fathers fell in Freedom's glorious strife,
God grant your chain of Union ne'er may nip—
　　Be brothers as you've been at Tennants' trip.

May Peace and Plenty ever o'er you smile;
　　Contentment makes a poor man feel a king;
And though you are the humble sons of toil,
　　May yours be Heaven, holy and serene,
When from your mortal coil you calmly slip,
　　Taking your last, your long immortal trip.

Lines to J. Y. L., Parkhead.

BROTHER of genius, son of song,
　　May thy heart ne'er feel a sorrow
Whilst thou'rt gaily journeying on,
　　Hailing hope each coming morrow.
Whilst life's rough battle thou dost brave,
May fame's gold banner o'er thee wave.

When through dreamland thou art straying,
　　Courting the sweet queen of muse;
Whilst thy brow she is arraying
　　With the gems her soul infuse,
Go and string thy love-fraught lyre
That's tuned with true poetic fire.

My best and truest friend is dead,
And with him love and joy have fled.

Then what avails my soaring soul
    When bowed myself unto the ground—
When galling chains of fate's control
    Still cauterize the bleeding wound,
That seeks in vain a healing balm
Its agonising pangs to calm?

Beloved bard, such is the lot
    Of her thou dost so highly prize;
Although too true, believe it not,
    But view me still with musing eyes,
A high-souled girl with gifted mind
The best of gentle womankind.

For long in sorrow have I sung,
    And still my wonted strains I'll sing
Until my harp it is unstrung
    And death hath soothed my suffering,
And then the world thy worth may see,
Neglected songstress of Dundee.

Lines

TO G. D. RUSSELL, LATE OF ST NINIAN'S, STIRLING,

WHO SAILED FROM LONDON FOR QUEENSLAND, NOVEMBER 18, 1865.

Thou art gone, perhaps for ever; oh, God! though thus we part,
'Tis death—only death—can sever thine image from my heart,
For mine eyes shall ever view thee where nature's beauty springs,
And my fancy shall pursue thee on love's bright golden wings.

Thou hast left me here in sorrow and sadness to repine,
With the golden hope to borrow that I am ever thine,
For thou hast most freely given thy noble loving heart,
And I have vowed to Heaven with it I ne'er shall part.

'Tis safe within my keeping and its trust I'll ne'er deceive;
Ah! blame me not for weeping, though 'tis all in vain to grieve.
Still I love thee unto madness—thou art twined in every thought,
And life can bring no gladness, my belov'd, where thou art not.

I loved thee ere I saw thee; a strange and mystic spell,
Like a spirit, moved within me, and language cannot tell
All the loving thoughts I nourished, the deep sincere regard
My blighted bosom cherished for St Ninian's noble bard.

When mine eyes are dim with weeping, my album then I bring,
When the weary world is sleeping on slumber's downy wing;
Then I turn its golden pages to gaze upon thy carte,
That's immortalised through ages, my own beloved bard.

But I dare not gaze upon thee—I feel my brain on fire—
Then I fling my album from me, and string my love-sick lyre;
But its songs are full of sorrow, no hope-stars from it spring—
It nameth not the morrow thy return shall gladness bring.

Oh! when shall I behold thee, and gaze upon thy face,
And when shalt thou enfold me to thy loving heart's embrace?
Through the winds so wildly swelling with dark December's breath,
I hear thee whisper Ellen, I am thine, yea, unto death.

I cannot—dare not doubt thee—I know thy heart is mine;
And though doomed to live without thee, my love and life are thine;
Where'er thy footsteps wander, whate'er thy lot may be,
Remember, George, remember, that I live to love but thee.

Lines to R. H. P., Parkhead.

In acknowledgment of his new-year's gift (duly received), a carte de visite, a lock of hair, and magnificent Bible, with the following inscription:—"Presented to Miss Ellen Johnston, by John Pettigrew (*alias* R. P. H., Parkhead), as a token of his respect and appreciation of her high literary talents. — Parkhead, 15th December, 1865."

DEAR much-loved friend, my swelling heart,
    It fain would sing a song of glee;
Oh, could my humble muse impart
    The gratitude I owe to thee,
I'd sing from morn till sunbeams set,
To pay thee back my honour'd debt.

May the gift that thou hast given,
    To prove thy heart's regard for me,
Lead my wand'ring soul to Heaven,
    Where I shall hope to meet with thee.
Shall kindred souls like thine and mine
In other spheres than Heaven shine?

Thy little carte, thy lock of hair,
    Within my locket I will place,
And next my heart I'll wear it there,
    With his whose name already grace
The golden page of glorious fame,
Whose heart no other maid can claim.

Tell me, my friend, what have I done,
    That I from thee those gifts have earned?
Thy love and sympathy I've won;
    Nay more, a secret I have learned—
I still have friends to show respect,
And lovers that will not me neglect.

How proud I feel this day to boast
    Of honour a princess might approve;
Since I sung for the Penny Post,
    Ah! mine has been a reign of love,
No fictitious tale of random chance,
But stern reality's romance.

When first to thee my muse I penned,
    That in its pages did appear,
I only had one single friend
    My lonely drooping heart to cheer;
But I have friends and lovers now
That to my very shadow bow.

I've found a friend I will not name,
    But leave the wond'ring world to guess;
It is his highest heartfelt aim
    For to promote my happiness.
Let every reader of the Post
Give him a happy new-year's toast

Both thee and him shall ever share
    In friendship's chain the golden part;
And when I breathe a fervent prayer
    For him to whom I gave my heart,
I'll pray that God may bless all three,
That many new-years each may see.

The Factory Girl's Address to her Muse.

SING on, my muse! With gladness give thy harp a cheerful tone.
Why thus repine in sadness, when no longer thou'rt alone?
Bid those hopeless feelings slumber and soothe thy cares to rest—
Kindred lovers without number long to fold thee to their breast.

Though humble be thy station, still a charm thou dost impart
To swell with admiration full many a noble heart;
From both village, town, and city love songs are sung to thee,
Yet thou could'st not melt to pity the heart of sweet Dundee.

When her banners they were waving from towers of self-built fame—
When her bonnets they were craving new honours for her name—
Though she knew thy heart was bleeding while bending o'er thy loom,
She heard thee, but unheeding all, she left thee to thy doom.

She knew thou wert a stranger and an orphan without home,
But thou shalt yet avenge her, for the time ere long will come
When thou'lt pay her retribution for sorrow, tears, and woe,
And the deep-dyed persecution which thou didst undergo.

From lands far o'er the ocean the harp of mansion-hall
Responds with deep devotion to thy love-sick wailing call;
The lonely peasant bendeth o'er his harp so long unstrung,
His lyric gifts he sendeth for the songs that thou hast sung.

Ah! long hast thou been sighing o'er thy youth's blighted bloom,
Like the desert flower when dying amidst its own perfume,
With no eye to prize its beauty save God's who gave it birth—
None to hail with love-born duty the fragrance of its worth.

Long has thy struggle lasted with stern Fate's galling strife,
When weary and exhausted, thine own hand would sever'd life;
Behind the dark cloud covering thy dark despairing doom
Yon radiant sun was hovering that's dawning through the gloom.

Then wouldst thou sit repining in this bright heaven-born hour,
When thy nation's heart is twining hope-stars around thy bower,
When old Scotland's bards are stringing love-pearls round thy brow,
And friendship's flowers are springing to greet thee with their bow?

Art thou not crowned an empress of soul-inspiring theme—
A fair and beauteous poetess—thine own bard's angel dream?
Could more honour'd names be given to thee beneath the sun,
Save to style thee Queen of Heaven—a name none ever won?

Art thou worthy of those honours that are bestowed on thee?
Or hast thou witched the donors with some mystic minstrelsy,
That long slumb'ring harps awaken to sound from shore to shore
Thy name, with fame unshaken, which thou never heard'st before?

Would'st thou change thy crown of glory, jewelled with golden
    fame,
Immortalised in story with a never-dying name?
Would'st thou part that lyric pearl that shines upon thy brow,
Thou call'st The Factory Girl, for thy sovereign's sceptre now?

Ah! sing on, my muse, with gladness strain thy harp's every
    chord;
Thou hast fought, yea unto madness, thy pen has been thy sword;
From the field thy foes are driven, and victory is thy boast,
Give thanks to God in Heaven, and the far-famed Penny Post

Lines to Mr Colin Steel,

FROM HIS OLD SCHOOLMATE AND COMPANION 'THE FACTORY GIRL.'

Dear schoolmate of my childhood years,
    Companion of those sunny hours,
Long ere mine eyes were dimmed with tears,
    Or weeds had sprung in place of flowers—

Hours when this heart ne'er knew a care,
    Save when thy absence chilled each thought,
I still felt glad when thou wert there,
    But ah! how sad when thou wert not.

Oft have I sat on Glasgow Green
    And wove with joy my daisy chains,
Then sought thee that they might be seen—
    Thy smiles were payment for my pains.

Ah! how I loved thee, Colin Steel—
    Thou wert my first, my childhood love—
At jingo-ring I would reveal
    Thou wert the lad I would approve.

When gazing on life's retrospect,
    Those gladsome childhood's days I see—
How vividly I recollect
    Those joyous hours I've spent with thee!

Yea, every scene springs up to view
    As if I gazed upon them still—
The schoolhouse, and the dyehouse too,
    The churchyard, and the old silk-mill.

Though many a year hath fled since then,
    And grief hath wrapt my soul in gloom,
Those early scenes inspire my pen—
    I feel like maiden in youth's bloom.

But, ah! how dim my bright blue eye,
    Care-clouds are wreathed around my brow!
My cheeks have lost their rosy dye,
    My flaxen hair is darken'd now.

In after years a lover came,
    His heart was wrapt in dark deceit;
He cast a shadow o'er my name,
    And left me then in grief to weep.

And ne'er while life my heart runs through
    Can I such joy or pleasure feel,
Or love with love so pure and true,
    As childhood's love for Colin Steel.

The Sha'maker's Wife.

Ye sons o' St Crispen, listen tae me,
And a story I'll tell, I vow it's nae lee,
Its like was ne'er heard in the toon o' Dundee—
    It's concerning a sha'maker's wife.

She ne'er was at rest frae morning till e'en,
Aye stirring up strife and brewing at spleen,
Lang ere the cock crew or daylicht was seen,
    She was raging—this sha'maker's wife.

In a wee Verdant factory she toiled for her bread,
For her manie he swore by his rosit-end-thread
He wad ne'er sew a shae sic a limmer to feed,
    As his gossiping trolloping wife.

In this bonnie wee factory ae fine summer day
Unto some o' her neebors this she did say—
'When the poetess passes at her we'll hurra;
    Will we no?' said the sha'maker's wife.

'We'll shout rhyming Nell, and mak' her feel mad,
And up at oor gate we'll stick a big flag,
Then at dinner-time we'll carry the jad';
    What think ye?' said the sha'maker's wife.

Twa jist like hersel', wi' Satan aye thrang,
Wi' a turkey red napkin a flag they did plan;
Three red and white tassels doon frae it hang,
    Roon the lugs o' the sha'maker's wife.

The flag it was hoisted wi' glory and pride,
And the passers-by thocht it for some bonnie bride,
So they lined up the street in a file, side by side,
    Crying—'Weel din, braw sha'maker's wife.'

As Nelly drew near she heard a great yell,
She asked at a kimmer—'What's yon, can ye tell?'
'It's a flag they've got up for you, rhyming Nell,
    It was hoist by the sha'maker's wife.'

'A flag up for me; I'll flag them,' said Nell;
'I'll gie them a flagging they winna like well
Wi' a lash o' tongue leather nae merchant can sell,
    And I'll cobble the sha'maker's wife.

Nell vowed by the sea, the Tay, and the tide,
That ere the sun set on the sweet banks o' Clyde
She wad fa' on a plan to settle the pride
    O' the meddling sha'maker's wife.

Awa Nelly flew in a rapture sublime,
Drank ae glass o' rum punch wi' the goddess o' rhyme;
If I'm no mista'en, ye've heard ere this time
    How she flagged the sha'maker's wife.

Ye sons o' St Crispin, noo I will end,
My story's as true as ever was penned,
And I hope, frae my heart, I dinna offend
    The spouse o' the sha'maker's wife.

The British Lion.

Poodle doodle doo, cried the blessed baby's dog,
When he was done with dinner and had swallowed up a frog,
I am not satisfied while another it is frying,
I will go and pass the time, and I'll fight the British lion
        With my poodle doodle doo!
        Come on, you mighty lion,
        And show what you can do
        With your bow wow wow.

The dog began to bark and the lion he did bellow—
How dare you look at me, you usurping little fellow?
The dog faced the lion, his moustache all greased with tallow,
The lion caught his prey and the little dog did swallow
   With his poodle doodle doo!
   Come on now, cried the lion,
   And show what you can do
   With your bow wow wow.

The lion gave a grin, and when the little dog went down
He gazed on kingdoms three, famed for glory and renown;
He couldn't count their armies, their navy and their cannon,
Britain is well fortified, in that there is no gammon
   With my poodle doodle doo!
   She has swallowed me alive,
   And nothing can I do
   With my bow wow wow.

Auld Dunville.

You sons o' toil, wha like a glass,
In comfort, joy, and socialness,
Wha gie nae mair nor tak' nae less
   Than keeps ye richt,
It's you I mean for tae address
   In rhyme this nicht.

I ken there's mair folk in Dundee
Wha likes a glass as weel as me;
I'll no include the great T.-T.
   Association,
For weel I ken hoo I will dree
   Their condemnation.

But what care I, they ne'er can school
My reason up tae such a rule
Tae drink 'winnike,' cauld and foul,
   And gorge my wame
As if I was a water pool
   Or sewer's drain.

Gie me ae glass o' auld Dunville,
Jist o' the Rabbie Burns' style,
Pure as it comes frae Erin's Isle,
   Wi' noucht but water;
It winna set ye in a broil
   Nor on the batter.

There's naething in't tae bite your mou',
Tae make ye sick or like tae spue,
Tho' ye wad drink till ye got fou
   And nearly deid,
Ye winna rise wi' deevils blue
   Crammed in your heid.

It's brewed into a muckle vault,
Distilled frae guid auld Irish malt.
Oor London lords, may fame exalt
   Their royal name;
It's patronised without a fault,
   And used by them.

And mair than that, the Queen hersel'—
If a' be true that I've heard tell—
Has preed a drap and liked it well
   As weel's her lords;
And whiles she takes a gentle smell
   When need accords.

Lang may she bask in pleasure's smile,
Within the throne o' Britain's isle;
May sorrow ne'er her joy beguile,
  Nor blast her wealth,
And wi' ae glass o' auld Dunville
  I'll pledge her health.

Here's tae ye, England's bonnie Queen,
Yours is a reign o' peace serene—
Nae royal monarch ere has been
  Belov'd sae true,
And generations yet unseen
  Shall think on you.

O Come awa', Jamie.

O come awa', Jamie, and gie us mair licht,
We ken it's yer aim for to keep us a' richt,
For oor tenters, the rascals, they think it nae sin
O'er a half-cocked meter to wark us a' blin'.

We're aye glad to see ye come into the place,
A glint o' yer bonnet brings smiles to oor face,
And many a time for you we hae sorrit,
And prayed for gude luck to send us in Dorrit.

Oh! what was the use for new burners tae get,
And keep scarcely an inch o' licht in each jet;
For the yarn that we hae, a 'saint' wid harass,
And it's mair loss than profit heining the gas.

Tae weave jute in darkness is eerisome toil,
And far mair than a' that the work we maun spoil;
The jute roots like heather come into the camb,
And the yarn fa's awa' like tow in oor hand.

So, come awa, Jamie, and gie us full 'coke;'
Tae gie 'weavers' half-anes ye ken it's nae joke;
We'll gie ye a 'Donald'* some nicht though we borrit,
And lang may ye licht up the Chapelshade, Dorrit.

Nelly's Lament for the Pirnhouse Cat,
KILLED BY THE ELEVATOR, C——E FACTORY, DUNDEE.

Oh! fare-ye-weel my bonnie cat,
Nae mair I'll smooth yer skin sae black.
Mony a time I stroked yer back,
  Puir wee creator;
Ye've gane yer last lang sleep tae tak'.
  The Elevator

Has sent ye aff tae your lang hame,
Whaur hunger ne'er will jag yer wame,
Whaur ye shall ne'er put in a claim
  For meal or milk;
Yer in the 'pond,' free frae a' blame,
  Boiled like a whelk.

Puir hapless beast, what was't that took
Ye hunting into yon dark nook?
Whaur 'Death' sat cooring wi' his hook
  Tae nip yer neck.
I'll think upon yer deein' look
  Wi' sad respect.

* A glass of drink.

My very brain ran roon about
When I saw Archie tak' ye oot,
Wi' scalped pow and bluidy snoot.
   Heigh, when I think,
A stane tied roon yer neck, nae doot
    Tae gar ye sink.

Jist yesterday, my bonnie beast,
I held ye close unto my breast;
When, ye as proud as ony priest,
   Did cock yer lug;
Syne aff ye ran tae get a feast
    Frae yer milk mug.

But noo nae mair in oor pirnhouse
Ye'll hunt the rats, nor catch a moose,
Nor on the counter sit fu' douse,
   And mew and yell,
And shoot yer humph sae prude and spruce
    At rhyming Nell.

Your race upon the earth was ran,
Puir puss, ere it was weel began;
Ye've gane whaur beastie, boy, and man
   Are doomed tae go.
Omnipotence in His vast plan
    Ordained it so.

There's nane has deign'd tae mourn ye here,
Unless mysel' wi' grief sincere;
Though but a cat I'll still revere
   Thy worth wi' pity,
And ower yer memory drap a tear,
    Puir we cheetie.

A Satire on a Pretended Friend.

Your lordship mauna tak' it ill,
Though I this sheet o' paper fill
Wi' words that is as keen and snill
    As winter winds;
For it is sair against my will
    Tae write sic lines.

Though I hae scarcely pen or pence
This bitter sermon tae commence;
Tae tell the truth, my freen Pretence,
    I've but ae penny;
But, by my soul, I hae some sense,
    That's what ye ha'ena.

For if ye had ye micht hae seen
I never took ye for a freen,
Jist by the winking o' yer een,
    When ye were speaking,
Ye surely thocht that I was green,
    Or blin' wi' greeting.

Some folk that whiles gies you a ca',
I daurna name them for the law,
For they would clunch me in their claw,
    And try to hang me;
But if ye've ony brains ava,
    Ye'll understan' me.

Ilk inch o' me that they like weel,
They aff my banes richt sune could peel;
And tho' I was as black's the deil,
    They'd mak' me blacker;
Faith, they could drown me in a creel
    That held nae water.

My name they birrel roon yer table;
In truth, the same folk they are able
Tae mak' the snaw as black's the sable,
  Their tongue's nae scandal;
When man and wife begins tae dabble,
  Short burns the candle.

But since they've tramped upon my corns,
And gien me room tae show my horns,
I'll let them hear some thunder storms,
  See lichtening's dart;
Ae lash o' my tongue fu' o' thorns
  Will mak' them smart.

Although on me ye've turned your back,
And joined in wi' their leein' crack;
I'm sure I dinna care a plack
  For a' their taunting;
Gie them a glass or twa tae smack,
  That's a' they're wanting.

But if your ain words they be true,
Ten times I've heard it said by you
That 'poets' were made black an' blue
  By everybody,
An' called a guid-for-nothing crew
  O' Satan's study.

Were I as black as tongue could tell,
I'll be nae waur than your ainsel',
For ye are in the cursed spell
  O' Satan's verses,
And ye may never taste the well
  O' Heaven's mercies.

Noo, Sir, my sermon's at an end,
I carena though it should offend;
Ye've gien tae me ye may depend
    Much provocation.
I am your much offended friend,
    Of this dictation,   NELLY

Mrs Cooper.

OOR pirn wife's gane awa', Jamie,
    And we are unco sorry,
For weel we ken next week will bring
    An unco waesome story.
When weary waiting on oor pirns,
    In vain we a' will seek her,
And weel ye ken how we'll impose
    On Archie, Tom, and Peter.
    O dinna let her gang, Jamie,
        We canna dae withoot her,
    Tho' nane but Nell did miss the cat,
        We'll a' miss Mrs Cooper.

If you were there yoursel', Jamie,
    Tae len' a helping han',
It micht dae unco well, Jamie,
    Sae lang as you wad stan'.
But, oh, when ere you turned your back,
    Then wad come the hurry,
As if the deils were a' let loose
    Between Dundee and Kerrie.
    So dinna let her gang, Jamie,
        We canna dae withoot her,
    Tho' nane but Nell did miss the cat,
        We'll a' miss Mrs Cooper.

Wee Poet Nell.

Wee poet Nell made a sang on hersel',
　　Auld Lucky Neil said naebody boucht it,
But the truth for to tell, wee poet Nell
　　Hadna enouch to serve them that soucht it.

They came far and nigh Nell's sang for to buy,
　　They a' kent the muse her soul did inspire;
She made sangs sae weel that auld Lucky Neil
　　Said that she 'borrit,'—forgie the auld liar,

For wee poet Nell could baith buy and sell
　　Ane twice her size,—in truth, she's no canny,
Tho' oorit and black the wee jade could mak'
　　A sang an ell lang on Lucifer's grannie.

She ance made a sang upon a young man
　　Who listed, aye, true, he thocht sae much shame o't,
He said that she took her sangs frae a book;
　　But he got the profit—she got the fame o't.

Tho' she looks scanty she has got plenty,
　　It is nae for want she gangs aye sae bare;
She's mony a goon tae gang tae the toon,
　　A silk ane to tak' her to kirk or tae fair.

If I'm no mistaen, she's a house o' her ain,
　　Plenty o' bedding laid by for the making;
She's a clever wee body, he's waur than a cuddy
　　That winna tak' Nell—she's worth the taking.

If some folk be wise they'll tak' my advice,
　　And let wee poet Nell and poetry alane;
She'll ravel a pirn, will mak' their head turn,
　　Tae read it, I fear, wad puzzle their brain.

So noo, Lucky Neil, I'll bid ye fareweel,
    I think by this time I've got ye persuaded,
The sang in your nieve, ye'll surely believe—
    It was nae either ane but poet Nell made it.

The Peacock.

COME listen to me, ye Anderston folk,
And I'll tell unto you a comical joke;
Its moral is meant for the proud and the vain,
So I'll say naething ill if it is not ill taen.

In Scotland Street a peacock was bred,
A conceitier peacock its tail never spread;
They say a ship's beauty is when in full sail,
But this peacock's beauty lay all in its tail.

A peahen once promised this peacock to meet,
But somehow or other her tryst did not keep;
The next time they met it was crossing the Clyde,
The peacock spread his tail, and admired it with pride.

But the peahen addressed him, and to him did say—
'Don't look so high nor turn your head away,
For a prettier bird than ever you'll be,
I have disappointed for times two or three.'

But the cock spread his tail, his wings he did flutter;
He flew out of the boat and fell back in the water,
Then his head on the surface appeared like a mote,
And so loudly he crowed and grasped at the boat.

'O help, help!' he cried; 'if help is not soon found,
For that cursed peahen this day I'll be drowned.'
'Curse me not in thy wrath, the peahen,' she said,
'Where now is thy glory when thy feathers are laid?

What would it avail thee, thy beauty and pride,
Wert thou left here alone to sink in the Clyde?'
The peacock was drawn out and placed on the quay;
When he came to himself then attempted to flee.

The hen screamed and laughed till her eyes they grew blind,
To see his wet wings how they flapped in the wind.
So now I have ended this very true song,
And I hope, by doing so, I have not done wrong.

If you go to Houldsworth's great machine shop
You will have a chance to see that rare peacock;
And as for the hen, they have told unto me
That she's taken her roost somewhere in Dundee.

That before very long she will be a cock's bride,
But not to the peacock that crosses the Clyde.

The Fourpence Piece.

DEAR FRANCIS, take this fourpence piece
    That paid the car for me,
May it a thousand times increase
    When it returns to thee.
For I have blessed it o'er and o'er;
    A kiss on it I've prest;
With many thanks I now restore
    It back to Francis Best.

Were I to give my heart with it,
    That heart you might refuse;
I'll keep it until our next trip,
    And oft on it I'll muse.

If e'er we go a trip again,
    This shall be my request;
That my advice you'll not disdain,
    Now, listen, Francis Best.

Before we go another trip
    Twelve months must whirl round;
There's many a way in which you're fit
    To make this groat a pound.
Put it in a box to sleep;
    There let it quickly rest;
Add sixpence to it every week,
    And then, dear Francis Best,

When we all go to our next trip,
    This little box break up,
And you are sure to find in it
    A factory girl's luck;
And may you find a loving wife
    You can fold to your breast;
To see you happy still through life
    Is my wish, Francis Best.

Lines to Mr Alexander Campbell.

GOD spare thee long, my dearest friend,
    With hopes and joys to come,
And when thy journeying here doth end,
    May Heaven be thy home.

For thou hast made my earth a heaven,
    And chased away alloy;
My heart so long with sorrow riven
    Beats now with gladsome joy.

And thou hast strewn my path with hope,
    Until the past doth seem
A glimmering fancy in each thought,
    Or false delusive dream.

Ah! could I tell thee how I feel—
    Could I in language speak
My thoughts, when memory reveals,
    How often I did seek

A friend to save e'er I would sink,
    And do what thou hast done,
Thou wouldst not marvel though I think
    Thee more than mortal one.

And couldst thou know how I have wept
    O'er many a bitter wrong;
Oft when the weary world slept
    I've sung my sorrow-song.

And couldst thou gaze into my heart
    To read the history there,
How true to thee it would impart
    The weary load of care

That thou hast lifted from my soul
    The joy that I have found;
With hope's sweet balm thou hast made whole
    The hopeless, bleeding wound.

Through life thy name with deep regard
    Around my heart I'll twine,
And may kind Heaven thy deeds reward,
    And bless both thee and thine.

Lines to the Memory of a Beloved Wife.

Thou art gone my loved and loving,
    Thou hast vanished from this earth
Like an angel spirit moving
    Through the glory of its worth.
Though each coming morrow bringeth
    Dark shadows o'er my doom,
Thy hallow'd memory flingeth
    A sunshine o'er my gloom.

Thou sleep'st thy dreamless slumber
    In the gloomy vale of death,
My sighs thou canst not number,
    For still's thy balmy breath
That oft came stealing o'er me,
    And made my heart rejoice;
When care-clouds lowered before me,
    Thou dispelled them with thy voice.

The sun awakes in gladness,
    And hails the dark, blue sea;
But he cannot cheer my sadness,
    Nor bring back joy to me.
His golden crest is blazing
    On sweet Clutha's silvery wave,
Whilst sadly I am gazing
    On my Mary's silent grave.

Through fancy I behold thee
    Still blooming in thy pride,
As when first I did enfold thee,
    My lovely chosen bride,
When I led thee from the altar
    In the happy long-ago,
With love that ne'er did falter,
    Still the same in joy or woe.

All in vain now I deplore thee,
    And heave the burning sigh,
For I never can restore thee
    From thy home beyond the sky.
I know thou'rt there, my Mary,
    Thy spirit beckons me,
And bids me not to tarry,
    But haste and come to thee.

When my last sad task is ended
    In this world of busy strife;
When my dust with thine is blended,
    My dear, beloved wife,
The world shall tell my story,
    When death this form enfold
In literary glory,
    Where my name was long enrolled.

Fare-thee-well, my gentle Mary,
    I'll see thy form no more;
Glide past me like a fairy
    Of dreamland's sunny shore.
When life's silver links are riven,
    Oh may we meet on high,
In the bright realms of Heaven
    Beyond the starry sky,
Where love can never die.

An Address to my Brother Bards.

Sing on, my brother bards to me,
    Your sweet enchanting strains
Has charmed me with their melody,
    And burst the captive chains

That bound my weary soul for years,
    And dimmed my once bright eyes;
That paled my rosy cheek with tears,
    And rent my heart with sighs.

I cannot speak the thoughts that spring
    Within my grateful heart,
And yet I ask you still to sing,
    Such joys you can impart;
Though I possess no golden dower,
    Nor wealth to me belongs,
My glowing heart shall ever shower
    Sweet blessings o'er your songs.

I am not now what once I was,
    A creature of neglect;
My country's love upholds my cause,
    And regards me with respect.
A band of glorious bards arise
    And lend to me their aid;
Their love-songs echo in the skies
    Whilst envy shrinks dismayed.

My trampled rights are now restored,
    And honour jewels my name;
My captive muse afar hath soared
    On wings of golden fame.
She flies before the world unmasked,
    Unfettered now and free;
Spontaneous warriors unasked
    Fought for her liberty.

She cannot lose her lustre now,
    Nor darken 'neath the blaze
Of those bright gems twined round her brow
    Your harps wove in her praise.

Those gems that never can grow dim,
    Whose glory ne'er can die,
But live like the stern patriot's hymn
    In fame's immortal sky.

Sing on, my brother bards, to me,
    Through centuries yet unseen,
Your glorious names of minstrelsy
    Shall bloom for ever green.
Old Scotland shall feel proud ere long,
    When time your worth unfurl,
That she you crowned the Queen of Song
    Was but a Factory Girl.

An Address to Nature on its Cruelty.

O NATURE, thou to me was cruel,
That made me up so small a jewel;
I am so small I cannot shine
Amidst the great that read my rhyme.
When men of genius pass me by,
I am so small they can't descry
One little mark or single trace
Of Burns' science in my face.
Those publications that I sold,
Some typed in blue and some on gold,
Learned critics who have seen them
Says origin dwells within them;
But when myself perchance they see,
They laugh and say, 'O is it she?
Well, I think the little boaster
Is nothing but a fair impostor;
She looks so poor-like and so small,
She's next unto a nought-at-all;

Such wit and words quite out-furl
The learning of " A Factory Girl." '
At first they do my name exalt,
And with my works find little fault;
But when upon myself they gaze,
They say some other claims the praise.
O Nature, had'st thou taken time
And made me up somewhat sublime,
With handsome form and pretty face,
And eyes of language—smiles of grace;
With snowy brow and ringlets fair,
A beauty quite beyond compare;
Winning the charms of fortune's smile.
Still dressed in grandeur all the while;
Then those who see me would believe
I never tried for to deceive
By bringing out a publication
Of borrowed lines or yet quotation.
But those who see me in this dress,
So small and thin I must confess,
Well may they dare the words to use.
Can such a vase distil Love's muse;.
Well may they ask dare I profess
The talent of an authoress?
Oh who could deem to gaze on me,
That e'er I mused on land or sea,
That I have sat in shady bower
Musing on thy fairest flower;
That I have sought the silvery stream
At midnight hour, calm and serene,
When skies of diamond sparkling flame
Shed pearly tears of heartsick shame,
To see me bound in hardship's blight,
Whilst man did rob me of my right,

And critics read my simple rhyme
And dared to say it was not mine?
Imperfect though my lays may be,
Still they belong to none but me.
My blighted breast is their abode,
They were placed there by nature's God;
And though my years are spent in pain,
Still seeking fortune's smiles in vain,
Still sighing youth's sweet years away,
Changing life's light into clay;
Hard toiling for my daily bread
With burning heart and aching head.
A vision of delusion's dream,
Hastening downward death's dark stream;
Yet nature between you and I,
Beneath the universal sky,
Who dares to say I have bereft
Another genius of their gift.

The Trip o' Blochairn.

Let them boast o' their trips that's given Scotland a name,
Engraved on the pages o' commerce and fame;
But amang a' their trips I'm happy to learn
There's nane has renown like the trip o' Blochairn.

There's something about them that brings me in min'
O' the warrior chieftains that conquered langsyne,
When oor patriot Wallace sae valiant and stern,
Hid amang the grey glens not far frae Blochairn.

Oor freen, William Riddle, his praise I will sing,
When he's mounted on horseback and dressed like a king;

His horse wi' a croon and his hat wi' a charm,
He's Wallace the Second at the trip o' Blochairn.

In Blochairn there's Englishmen—Irishmen tae;
But what Scotchman could look at Will Riddle's array,
And forget his forefathers that sleeps 'neath the fern,
That waves green on the hills at the back o' Blochairn?

They sleep in the soil whaur their bluid was embued,
But their spirits unseen has despotics subdued;
Nae usurping tyrant ever can govern
The century that reigns wi' the trip o' Blochairn.

For micht yields to richt, and gives honour her due,
And Britain's three kingdoms are a' sisters noo;
And freenship re-echoes frae mountain and cairn,
Love unfurls her flag at the trip o' Blochairn.

'Tis the flag that was woven by freedom's ain plan,
And it speaks o' the love between master and man,
Whilst tyranny creeps like a wee helpless bairn,
And is crushed 'neath their feet at the trip o' Blochairn.

O lang may Blochairn in commerce succeed,
May her sons aye be social whate'er be their creed;
May the dark demon care never cause them concern
While Riddle reigns king at the trip o' Blochairn.

POETIC ADDRESSES AND RESPONSES.

To the Factory Girl.

Sing on, sweet girl, chant forth thy cheering strain,
    And secret solace seek for saddened joy;
Thy harp's rich numbers Ninian's Bard might wean
    From wandering fortune 'neath a stranger sky.

But friends spring up, fair poetess, like flowers,
    Spontaneous beings of a summer day;
Attachment varies, but affection bowers
    And blooms aye freshest in its native air.

Thy melting melodies, thou emperess of song,
    From slumber's silent, lone, secluded cell
Hath woke the harp that, idly unstrung,
    Hung mute and tuneless on its cloister'd wall.

And Scotland's hills and rugged rocks shall ring,
    And Ellen's fame shall cleave the crested wave,
When thine own bard shall waft from Queensland strains
    Memorials of thy love in future lays.

Then mourn not, maid, 'tis madness to repine;
    And grief rings love from out young tender hearts,
Which turns upon itself inflicting pain—
    It tears the bandage from the bleeding smart.

How weak thy bard's effusions classed with thine,
    Tho' praise comes pleasant howsoe'er compiled!
'Tis merit gilds the poet's sacred shrine,
    And favour nurseth talent's orphan child.

Dumfries, Dec., 1865.   MAT. STEVENSON.

Lines

RESPECTFULLY DEDICATED BY DANIEL SYME, LANARK, TO THE FACTORY GIRL, DUNDEE.

There lives a maid in fair Dundee,
The licht o' a sweet bardie's e'e,
Wha labours hard in foreign soil
To win Dame Fortune's sunny smile,
Wha aft will pray that God may guide
And shield frae harm his promised bride.
Wha aft, when 'mid fair Queensland's bowers,
He whiles away the evening hours,
Will sing wi' pride the lofty lays
Soul-stirring bards wrote in her praise.
But louder yet her praise they'll sound,
And tell that maid whom friends disowned—
'The Factory Girl'—whom fate severe
Hath caused to shed the bitter tear,
Has Scotland's favourite become,
And struck her foes with wonder dumb.
Long live the maid, long live the swain!
May fair winds waft him back again!
Then filled thy cup o' bliss shall be
Thou beauteous warbler o' Dundee.

To the Factory Girl.

Dream on, dear girl, I am ever thine—
  Nought can estrange this heart from thee;
Thy image in my heart doth shine—
  I ne'er shall prove untrue to thee.

For thee alone, my Ellen dear,
    And dear old Scotia's mountains blue,
My heart shall beat without a fear,
    Knowing that thou art ever true.

And when the happy time arrives
    That I shall press my lips to thine,
And I shall gaze into those eyes
    That sparkle with a light divine,

Then thou shalt know my heart was true
    Before I saw thy form divine;
When first I spake of love to you
    I was and shall be ever thine.

St Ninian's, Stirling.   G. D. RUSSELL.

A Farewell Address.

WRITTEN BEFORE LEAVING FOR QUEENSLAND.

My native land I canna lea,
My hame an' a' that's dear to me;
I canna gang ayont the sea
    Wi' easy mind—
I canna stray, dear land, from thee,
    As I were blind.

Nor can I gaze on hill an' lea,
On meadow green, or flower, or tree;

And these, when thou art hid from me,
        Chase from my mind
My dearest thoughts, dear land, to thee,
        Their way shall find.

I would not leave thy seabound shore,
For leaving thee my heart is sore;
But when fate's hand is on the oar
        We canna flee,
Nor need we think to pass the door
        Of destiny.

So, fare-thee-well my high-souled land,
Thou land of landscapes wild and grand;
Thine is the honour to command
        A glorious name,
Thy privileged sons to wield the wand
        Of honoured fame.

And you, my fast and truest friends,
Whose cheering influence pleasure lends,
Whose friendship aye so largely tends
        To lighten care;
A fond adieu! One prayer spend—
        That well I fare.

Farewell my hame—my good old mother,
My more than friend—my dearest brother,
Farewell my brothers altogether—
        Aye brithers be;
And girl more dear than summer weather,
        Farewell to thee.

St Ninian's, Oct. 28, 1865.   G. D. RUSSELL.

To the Factory Girl.

Hail, princess o' the poetic race,
I lang tae see thy comely face,
Thou'rt worthy o' the highest place
    In fame's gay tower;
In thee I do a writer trace
    O' wondrous power.

Sweet poetess, 'twould indeed be hard
Wert thou forgot on thy native sward;
Our Queen thy merits did regard
    With due respect;
Then why should I, a humble bard,
    Thy worth neglect?

Let Scotia's sons and daughters fair
From out their funds subscribe a share,
All those that can a half-crown spare
    Will be well paid
While musing o'er thy beauties rare,
    High-gifted maid.   R. H. P.

To the Factory Girl.

The melody of thy sweet muse
    Has waked my sleeping lyre,
And in my very heart and soul
    Has kindled a desire

To bid my humble muse arise
    And sing with heartfelt glee
The praises of the Factory Girl
    Who dwells in sweet Dundee.

Sing on, thou sweet enchantress, sing,
    Thy muse shall higher soar—
Thy fame shall spread o'er Britain's isles,
    And cross to India's shore.

Then why repine whilst at thy loom,
    Amidst the factory din?
Thou'rt weaving for thyself a name;
    Bright honours thou shalt win.

The lustre of thy muse shall shine,
    And stamp its image bright,
On minor poets yet unborn,
    And fill them with delight.

O, thou sweet poetess, accept
    This humble lay of mine;
Were I endow'd with powers like thee,
    I'd make it brighter shine.
                  PETER M'CALL.

GEORGE STREET, AYR, Jan. 23, 1866.

To the Factory Girl.

WHEN last I wrote the muse was shy,
And wi' a nod jist passed me by,
An' since she's gane I seldom try
    Poetic strife;
But whistling mak' the shuttle fly
    Tae please the wife.

In days o' yore, like poets vain,
I thocht the thing was a' my ain;
But faith I fin' I've been mista'en,
    And frankly tell,
I ne'er could sing a glowing strain
    Like bonny Nell.

I'm proud tae see a factory lass
The modern bardies a' surpass;
I'll buy her book if I hae brass,
  Be't cheap or dear,
An' read it ower a flowing glass,
  My heart to cheer.

Tae her I send nae tuft o' hair,
Nor sacred book wi' Davie's prayer;
But should she come tae Lanark fair,
  An' ca' on me,
I'll tak' her, wi' a brither's care,
  The Falls to see.

LANARK, Jan. 20, 1866. A FRIEND.

To the Factory Girl.

DEAR ELLEN, I have now sat down
 To write to thee in homely strain;
But ah! to add to thy fame's crown
 Would only be a task in vain.
Had I a gifted pen like thine,
 In fame's gay tower my name might bloom;
But ah! thy lays shall brightly shine
 When mine are 'neath oblivion's tomb.

'We've Parted' is a glorious gem;
 So is thy last farewell address;
Thy 'Pleasure Trip' doth crown thy pen,
 Thou soul-inspiring poetess.
I find, in looking o'er the past,
 Misfortunes thou hast had thy share;
But happiness has come at last—
 No more thou'lt give way to despair.

Thy absent lover is a treasure
    You say was partly won by me;
Oh! how it gives unbounded pleasure
    To know some good I've done for thee!
Thou shalt be foremost in my prayer,
    Whilst love and sympathy extend;
Even this humble 'lock of hair'
    May aid to show I am thy friend.

I wish thee joy with all my heart,
    Yet my thoughts I can't express;
And send this Bible as a mark
    Of how I prize the poetess.
And though I now take leave of thee,
    I still will hold thy memory dear.
Farewell, dear girl; may'st thou see
    Many a brilliant good new-year.   R. H. P.

NEW ROAD, PARKHEAD, Dec., 1865.

The Maid o' Dundee.

THE sun frae the east his bright radiance had flung
O'er the land where a Burns and a Tannahill sung,
When, musing, I wander'd on, on to the sea—
My thoughts deeply centred on bonnie Dundee.

Dundee's bonnie banners fu' proudly may wave,
And her bonnets be worn by the sons of her brave;
But her banners or bonnets are naething to me
Compar'd to the maiden o' bonnie Dundee.

The mavis at eventide fu' sweetly may sing,
Or the cooing o' doves make the woods a' to ring;
But their notes altogether sound harshly to me,
Compar'd to yon warbler frae bonnie Dundee.

Proud Ayrshire may boast o' her lasses sae braw—
Wi' cheeks like the roses, wi' broos like the snaw;
But what is their beauty?—'tis nothing to me,
When matched with thy charms, bonnie maid o' Dundee.

Far, far hae I wander'd old Scotland o'er—
Seen the mountain waves lashing her rocky east shore—
Heard her western winds sighing amid Craigielea;
But I ne'er saw a maiden sae lovely as thee.

Ah! had I but back the days that are gane,
When morn, noon, and eve I could roam a' alane,
There's nae joy on earth wad be dearer to me
Than to clasp to my bosom the maid o' Dundee.

Farewell, lovely maiden—farewell for a while;
May Heaven's choicest blessings around thee aye smile;
With joy I will mind to the day that I dee
The first time I heard o' the maid o' Dundee.

ANDREW DICKIE.

KILMARNOCK, Nov. 30, 1865.

To the Factory Girl.

FAIN would I know the gentle source
Which did thy infant soul inspire
With rapturous words, whose glowing warmth,
Year by year, is rising higher.

* * * * * *

Obscure at first a gem was hid
'Mid factory's dingy walls,
Whose glowing radiance might have decked
The noblest marble halls.
'Twas found at last, and deeply prized,
And lo! behold it now!

'Mid wreaths of fame it sparkles forth
Upon a maiden's brow.
With magic spell it gained esteem—
Love, honour, and renown—
And placed upon her youthful head
The poet's laurel crown.
And now triumphantly she stands
High on the height of fame;
That gem—her soul—still glittering adds
Fresh honours to her name.

D. STEWART KERR.

To the Factory Girl.

WITH the chill blast that sweeps from the snow-covered north
    Comes a strain of new music the sweetest
Ever woke up the pensive, turned sadness to mirth,
    Or dismissed a rude feeling the fleetest.

'Tis the purl of the stream, not the cataract hurled
    From the masculine brow ever clouded;
'Tis the ring of an angel's harp greeting the world,
    When a halo of peace would enshroud it.

'Tis the story of virtue, the music of love,
    From a high soul of industry smiling
At our callous neglect, though the graces approve
    And attend the fair poetess toiling.

Charming minstrel, sing on; o'er thy solitude cold
    Shall the slumbering genius of fame yet
Wake responsive to thine, and thy temples enfold
    With a diadem worthy thy name yet.

H. SMITH.

GLASGOW, March, 1866.

Lines to Mr J. Smith, Glasgow.

BORNE thence on the wings of green spring's balmy breath,
    A brave minstrel's sweet song is rebounding
From the land where my forefathers slumber in death—
    'Tis a song in my praise he is sounding.

And he sings in the land—that gay city of fame,
    Where industry her garlands is twining;
Where the muse like a rainbow encircles my name,
    Like a star in the firmament shining.

Tis the land where all those I loved best, on earth
    Sleep in death, yea, for ever departed
To that land whence again they can never bring mirth
    To this bosom they left broken-hearted.

And though lovers and friends have sprung up in their stead,
    Yet how sad and how sceptic the feeling
When compar'd with the flame that I fanned for those dead,
    When my young heart its trust was revealing.

I may love and be loved still as deep and as dear,
    With a heart of affection o'erflowing,
But the spell-binding charm no longer is near
    That I felt in my young bosom glowing.

The gold garlands of fame may entwine round my brow,
    And the dark clouds of sorrow keep waning,
And the god of the muses in homage may bow,
    And the future bring gold for the gaining;

But the love that I feel for my dear native land,
    Where I rambled in childhood so cheery,
It can never grow cold until Death's icy hand
    Leads me through his dark valleys so dreary.

Oh, Glasgow, dear Glasgow, thou sweet home of my youth,
    Land of labour and love's swelling story;
Ah! thou land of my kindred, believe me, in truth,
    Thou art old Scotland's temple of glory.

Lines by Edith to the Factory Girl.

They ask me, girl, what made thee sing
    'Mid din of shuttle and of loom—
'Mid steam and dust and ceaseless ring
    Of cotton wheels in factory room.

What made thee sing? Ask first the thrush
    That haunts the woods 'bove fair Dundee,
And on her hills the breezes hush
    Till bird and breeze explain to me.

Hail, Spirit of the Golden Muse!
    Thou soul of beauty, that dost fill
The earth, and air, and dost diffuse
    On some thy soft revealings still.

That spirit taught thee, girl, to sing;
    She came to thee when early May
Doth first her golden shadow fling
    Upon the broad blue Frith of Tay;

She came what time the summer wood
    Bursts glorious into leaf and bower;
And oft she came in holier mood,
    At moonlit eve, or Sabbath hour.

And came she ne'er in love, first love,
    With whispers soft of some dark eye,
Whose gleam had flashed thy path above,
    Like meteor gem in life's young sky?

Came she not, too, in sorrow's shroud—
    What poet knows her not so dressed?—
Only to point the silver cloud,
    And whisper dreams of days more blest?

Sing on, young heart, of all that's fair
    Upon the banks of winding Tay;
The old grey towers, the blossoms there
    May mingle well in poet's lay.

When gazing on life's boundary hill,
    Thine eye at length doth long for rest,
Sing even then, thy numbers fill
    With chords more grand, with hopes more blest.

The Factory Girl's Reply to 'Lines by Edith.'

They ask thee, Edith, why I sing
    'Mid factory din, its dust and gloom,
And why I soar on fancy's wing
    'Mid dreamland bowers and summer's bloom.

Tell them the spirit bids me sing
    That made my soul, when but a child,
Enraptured with the budding spring,
    When wandering Cathkin's green woods mild.

While yet a child, scarce six years old,
    Musing on nature's carpet sod,
Among the fields like waving gold,
    I prized the works of nature's God.

Though little of His laws I knew,
    Yet still I felt their power supreme,
And loved His wondrous works to view,
    And chose them for my childish theme.

But time and tide flew on apace,
    And I was wafted from those scenes,
Borne thither to a sweeter place
    Near Kelvin's lovely crystal streams.

And still that spirit round me clung,
    And bound me in its mystic spell,
While fairy songs to it I sung
    When sitting by the Three-tree Well.

But like the linnet in the linn
    That's caught and caged in prison air,
They forced me midst the factory's din
    To chase my fairy phantoms there.

But still that spirit lingered near,
    And clasped my form so young and weak,
And kissed away the burning tear
    That scorched the rose-bloom on my cheek.

Then first love came with golden smiles—
    Sweet were the vows he did impart,
And with his false bewitching wiles
    He stole away my trusting heart;

Then left me with a look of scorn
    When he the seeds of grief had sown—
Wrecked in the bloom of life's young morn,
    Ere scarce her infant buds were blown.

Yet still I sung, though all in vain,
    While year in sorrow followed year,
When all at once like magic strain
    My harp burst on the world's ear.

Ah, gentle Edith, see me now,
    With hope's bright banner o'er me spread,
Fame's golden wreath around my brow,
    Love's lyric crown upon my head.

Dear Edith, they had hearts like thine
    Who wove that wreath and wrought that crown,
And built for me that glorious shrine
    That rears its tower on high renown.

Edith, farewell; may joy be thine!
    Perchance with thee I yet may meet,
When I shall press thy hand in mine,
    My kindred sister's love to greet.

Edith's Reply to the Factory Girl.

MAIDEN, well pleased the other day,
    I saw thy sister-hearted song,
And marked the music of the lay,
    Which grace to mine doth not belong.

I love thy life so sad, so sweet;
    Car'st thou to read stray leaves of mine?
Insipid they most eyes to meet,
    Perchance may favour find in thine.

Maiden, I was a lonely child;
    No sister played among the flowers
That grew within the green woods wild,
    Or blossomed in our garden bowers.

My earliest home was in a vale,
    Near where the Scottish Esk its waves
Doth mingle in the sea, whose gale
    Did kiss our flowers and churchyard graves.

A church with deep, deep tolling bell,
    A manse with ivy on its wall,
And shady trees where evening fell,
    Are earliest scenes I can recall.

I had a sire, not like to thine;
    He taught me first to love the muse
In 'jovial Junes' when roses twine,
    And birds their summer song diffuse.

He wandered oft alone with me
    Where grew the violet and primrose—
A solitary man was he,
    Whose lofty brow was thought's repose.

That brow I cannot paint, nor tell
    When first the grey hairs scattered there;
Through mental toil those silvers fell,
    Less due to years than unto care.

Some trace the lightning's rapid wing—
    The subtle elements of space,
And flowers of air and water bring
    In human art to find a place.

Praised be their labour who have toiled
    For science so; not less is theirs
The mazy rings that thought hath coiled
    Who loose and clear the mist she wears.

Such toil for him had Fate assigned—
    A work that's oft misunderstood,
And, more to blanks than prize resigned,
    That race ran he in patient mood.

Such was my childhood, such my sire;
    Since then, through years that swift did pass,
The Muse would oft my thoughts inspire—
    In schooldays, sometimes in the class;

In holiday, on banks of Clyde,
    Where shadows o'er the white Cloch creep,
Resting 'mong hills that blue lochs hide,
    Cradling their waves in sunny sleep.

'Then "First Love" came in golden dreams,'
　　As morn in Oriental clime;
Through vines and flowers a glory streams
　　That dies ere yet it be noontime.

Her beam, in memory lingering still,
　　Dear maid, doth cast o'er life a charm,
And points a heaven above earth's ill,
　　Where love doth dwell without alarm.

A world of beauty and of song,
　　Maiden, be thine; and the rich page
That doth to Poet's eye belong
　　Be still thy golden heritage.

Well did'st thou read its shining leaves,
　　With streaming eyes, thou artless child,
Beside the 'Three-tree Well,' on eves
　　Of summers gone and autumns mild.

Hail, Book of Nature! fairest sweet
　　Distilled from moonbeam and from flower
O'er thee Earth's weeping ones may meet,
　　And rest in pitying angel's bower.

To the Factory Girl.

HARK! ye lovers of the muse,
I hear a strain upon the gale;
The notes sound like the melody
Of him who sings at Calderyale.

But hark! a sweeter strain I hear;
I wonder whose song that may be?
A voice replied both loud and clear,
'Tis from the maid of sweet Dundee.

The gift of song once more returns
Back to Scotland's favoured isle;
She brings with her the harp of Burns
To cheer your harps but for a while.

Clear and sonorous be my strain,
Beneath her shade I frankly bow:
To sing her praise I'm doubly fond,
For I am all enchanted now.

She styles me bard of Caldervale—
Delighted name, if that were true!
I'll waft my songs upon the gale,
And try to imitate her, too.

Long may she shine as polar star,
When sable night her curtains hing;
He who dares her song to mar
Knows not the joy the muse can bring.

He who makes the flowers to grow,
And paints them with unerring skill,
Hath made a woman's strains to flow
Sweet as soothing Tannahill.

While morning dew as pearls appear,
While larks chant sweet on fluttering wings,
I'll keep an open, listening ear,
And stop my harp when Helen sings.

Rejoice, ye women of our land—
Ye maidens fair, and mother's too!
A Factory Girl can now command
The power of song possessed by few.

I leave my strain upon the world—
O may it wing its flight afar!
Her banner yet may be unfurled,
When Fame begins to drive her car.

MOFFAT.   DAVID MORRISON.

The Factory Girl's Reply to Edith.

HAIL! spirit of the gifted Nine,
    Again I call my humble muse
Her frail power in response to thine
    A weak and charmless song infuse.

Inspiring spirit, thy lofty lays
    A mystic witchery o'er me fling:
'Tis thee, not I, who claims the praise—
    'Tis of thy worth the world should sing.

The language that pervades thy songs
    Pourtrays a noble soul sublime,
And marks that worth to thee belongs
    I ne'er shall own through endless time.

Edith, beloved one, be it so;
    I love those sweet stray leaves of thine,
And feel what poets only know
    When kneeling by fair poesy's shrine.

'Twas on the banks of winding Esk,
    That murmurs by the Pentland Hills,
Thy sire taught thee thy glorious task,
    Whose golden number richly fills

Thy noble soul and nobler heart—
    Ah, Edith, false, false would they be,
Who would to me the palm impart
    That e'er had read thy minstrelsy.

Thy childhood's home stood in a vale,
    Where balmy breath of fragrant flowers,
Borne on the summer evening gale,
    Oft kissed its ivy-woven towers.

And there thou strayed a lonely child,
    Amongst the honey-suckle bowers,
Through foliage of the greenwoods wild,
    As onward flew youth's golden hours.

Then First Love came like angel queen,
    In robes of gold and tinsell'd maze;
Scarce ere thou hadst her beauty seen,
    She fled from thy enraptured gaze.

Such is too oft the poet's doom—
    The flower he ever prizeth most,
Long ere his hope hath reached its bloom,
    He finds his gem for ever lost.

Thy father was a genius too,
    His brow was draped with silver hair;
Ere Father Time's iron stamp was due,
    Deep thought had left her impress there.

A father's love I never knew,
    He left me when an infant child,
And sailed Columbia's shore to view,
    And chase ambition's fancy wild.

He was a bard—'tis from his veins
    That my poetic blood doth flow;
His were the wild and mystic strains
    Such as in Byron's breast did glow.

Eight years on Time's iron wings had fled,
    When Hope's gold star began to wane;
My mother, dreaming he was dead,
    Joined in wedlock's band again.

The grief that I have borne since then
    Is only known unto the Lord:
No power of words nor author's pen
    My countless wrongs can e'er record.

Another dozen years had fled:
 One day a startling letter came—
O God! my father was not dead,
 But living in the State of Maine.

Edith, I scarce dare tell thee more,
 Save where the Niagara's wave
Swells proudly o'er its pebbly shore,
 And points a suicide's sad grave.

Conscience wrung with wild remorse
 To hear his child, far-famed in song,
Wept 'neath a cruel stepfather's curse,
 That he himself had caused the wrong.

Whilst brooding o'er his past neglect,
 He felt no more a wish to live;
To close the sickening 'retrospect,'
 He took the life he could not give.

Such was my sire, and such his end,
 And such an end was nearly mine;
But Heaven its mercy did extend,
 And sent kind friends to save in time.

Edith, my heart's warm love is thine,
 In kindred soul and kindred thought:
Oh may we at our Saviour's shrine
 Obtain that love which faileth not!

The Factory Girl's Reply to David Morrison,
CALDERVALE, AIRDRIE.

Sing on, sweet bard of Calder plains,
 Oh, sing thy songs of wonted glee,
Thou hast enchanted with thy strains
 The Factory Girl of Dundee.

Hail! son of song, thou may'st not boast
  Of titled name nor classic lore;
But still thou hast a higher toast
  To spread thy name o'er Scotia's shore.

Thine is the pure, spontaneous muse
  That flows from nature's swelling spring,
And doth a heaven-born light diffuse
  O'er every heart that hears thee sing.

Sing on, sweet bard, where Calder flows—
  Where grandeur reigns and beauty springs,
And where the dew-kissed opening rose
  Unfolds her leaves like angel's wings;

When twilight's golden shadows creep
  Like whispering spirits on the gale,
And feathered warblers calmly sleep
  Among the trees of Caldervale—

When Heaven's blue vault with starlights blaze,
  And golden moonbeams o'er thee shine,
Then sing the Factory Girl's praise:
  Her soul shall breathe response to thine.

May peace and love smile o'er thy hearth;
  May clouds of dark corroding care
Ne'er come to blight thy bosom's mirth,
  Nor leave her sting of sorrow there.

'Tis true that Genius rarely smiles
  Upon the wealthy of our lands;
She chooseth those who bravely toil
  With willing hearts and hardy hands.

Her chosen children then are we,
  So let us sing, my brother bard:
When death hath stilled our minstrelsy
  Our worth shall win its own reward.

To the Factory Girl.

Long may you sing, enchanting maid,
    You charm my heart beyond compare:
To sing your praise I'm not afraid,
    Although I'm destitute of lair.

We had a Burns, a Tannahill,
    A Hogg, beloved by Scotland too;
But showers of joy my bosom fill
    Whene'er I sit and think on you.

You sing so sweet of Kelvin's streams,
    And Cathkin's woods sae bonnie green;
'Twas there you wandered when a child,
    Enraptured with the summer scene.

When nature's fields with flowers are spread,
    And dew-drops deck the opening rose,
I'll sit within some fragrant shade
    And sing your praise where Calder flows.

'Tis not the wealthy that doth fill
    Our land with song and genius true;
Hogg was a shepherd on the hill,
    Burns was a ploughman at the plough.

Hale be your heart, sound be your mind;
    O, never fling your harp away:
Though some may prove to be unkind,
    Bear on and sing, for well you may.

I read your strains with fond delight;
    All Scotland yet shall boast of thee,
And hail you as a comet bright,
    Thou gifted girl of sweet Dundee.

May golden smiles your face adorn,
    O'er roses may your footsteps move!
May peace and pleasure dwell with thee
    Until you reach yon home above!

When all your strains on earth are past,
    And farewell bid to all that's dear,
I hope you'll sing that song at last
    Which far transcends all music here.

DAVID MORRISON.

Lines to the Factory Girl,

BY A GLASGOW LASSIE.

Had I been gifted, gentle maid,
    With half thy sweet poetic fire,
Then would I make the Muse my slave,
    And bid the heavenly-sounding lyre
Extol thy praise till none should be
So famed as Ellen of Dundee.

But Fate so willed that thou shouldst sing,
    And I mute list to thy sweet strains,
And thank kind Heaven for sending here—
    To dry our tears and soothe our pains—
A creature womanly and kind,
With gentle heart and sterling mind.

Thy pretty songs I always read
    With genuine feelings of delight,
And know none save a maiden pure
    So warm and tenderly could write.
Kind wishes to thy shrine I bring—
Wishes my only offering.

O call me sister, and I will
    Give deep, unselfish love away;
O call me sister, for, like thee,
    I weary toil from day to day,
And feel sharp worldly thorns each hour,
Yet gather, too, sometimes a flower.

Thou lovest—blush not, sweetest maid—
    The heart secured is worth thy keeping;
'Tis joy to know on foreign soil
    A manly heart is warmly beating
With love that distance cannot fade
For thee, his gifted Scottish maid.

Perchance thy face I ne'er may see;
    If cruel fate has so designed,
Fancy shall ever picture thee
    As gentle, beautiful, and kind.
Thine be a bosom free from care,
Thine be a brilliant bright career,
So fondly hopes thy friend, C. R.

The Factory Girl's Reply
TO 'A GLASGOW LASSIE.'

Sister, wilt thou excuse me for my seeming cold neglect?
Do not deem that I refuse thee my heart's sincere respect;
For of thee I have been thinking each day—nay, every hour
Thy muse I have been drinking like dew-drops from the flower.

Ah, believe me, gentle sister, my soul thou dost enthral;
As the ivy leaves doth cluster around the ruined wall,
So doth thy sweet revealings cling as closely round my heart,
With fond endearing feelings that words can ne'er impart.

Sister, why art thou mourning for bright poetic fire,
Whilst heavenly light is burning around thy mystic lyre?
Why midst oblivion's slumber dost thou linger lone and mute,
Whilst thou with golden numbers canst tune thy silvery lute?

O! how I love to listen to that melody of thine!
When the pearly dew-drops glisten around the lily's shrine,
When the Queen of Night unfurls her banners o'er the Tay,
'Tis then the Factory Girl doth chant thy love-born lay.

Sister, hast thou been slighted by him that gained thy heart?
Has thy young life's love been blighted, thy fond hopes torn apart?
I heard a sigh of sorrow in thy song of minstrelsy,
And this secret I will borrow—' Hast thou ever loved like me?'

Ah! I have loved to madness; yet strange this tale may seem,
That my heart hath ne'er known gladness save when in fancy's dream;
For my cup has still been flowing with bitter misery,
And, alas! there is no knowing when joy will come to me.

Though a noble heart is toiling for me on a foreign soil,
Yet stern fate may be beguiling this bosom all the while.
Though that heart is in my keeping, I might never win the hand;
There's a boundless ocean sweeping between me and Queensland.

Ah! dark thoughts like these come crowding like mist across my mind,
All my cherished hopes enshrouding with doubts and fears combined.
The future seems a mystery. Alas! I only know
That my life is one dark history of toil-worn heart-sick woe.

But I know, my gentle sister, that thou canst sympathise,
And my heart is beating faster as I gaze with dreaming eyes
On the hour that I shall meet thee, for sure that hour shall come,
When I shall fly to greet thee, wherever be thy home.

Now, adieu! my dearest sister of song and weary toil,
Sharp thorns thy heart may cluster, yet gather flowers the while;
May a brighter fate be given to thee beneath the sky,
And thy after lot be Heaven—so hopes thy friend, E. J.

To the Factory Girl.

I AM gone perhaps for ever, for 'tis God can only tell—
I may see thee no more, never, the girl I love so well;
But should Dame Fortune smiling stand, and should the fates ordain,
I'll hasten to my fatherland, and to thee, my love, again.

Keep up a steady heart, love, there is no cause for fear,
But trust unto that Power above who brought me safely here;
As sure as seasons pass away, as sure as kindred die,
So in its course shall come that day—our union day is nigh.

'Tis strange we've never met, though our hearts are fond and true.
You know I've left you with regret my fortunes to pursue;
Regret doth haunt me still, for I may thee ne'er behold;
Of love I cannot get my fill, nor thee to my bosom fold.

I ofttimes sit and ponder, and oft repeat your lines—
Your absence makes them fonder—they are like so many shrines,
Where, when my heart is sore, I'll to solitude repair,
And at them pay my true devoir, and think thou sit'st there.

In this land of cloudless skies, and land of bushy wold,
Where spreading vineyards rise, where regions lie untold,
My aims might be aspiring, and vain the keen contest;
But with thee I'll soar untiring, and with success be blest.

Wilt thou be my happy bride,
    And keeper of my heart, love?
Wilt thou be my joy and pride
    Until death doth us part, love?
Wilt thou share my crooked lot,
    In sorrow or in joy, love?
And welcome any earthly spot,
    Or high or low employ, love?
Wilt thou cross the rolling sea,
    And come and dwell with me, love?
And you'll be all in all to me,
    And I'll be kind to thee, love.
For by the stars that gem the sky
    Far in infinite space, love,
Before their Maker, God on high,
    Save thee, I'll none embrace, love!
Thou art my light, my life, my all,
    The steerer of my fate, love!
O, listen to my eager call:
    Come o'er, no longer wait, love.

G. D. RUSSELL.

3 GREGORY TERRACE, FORTITUDE VALLEY, BRISBANE,
QUEENSLAND, AUSTRALIA, March 16, 1866.

Lines to Mr G. D. Russell, Queensland,

ACCOMPANIED WITH A CARTE DE VISITE OF 'THE FACTORY GIRL'

SAY not, dear George, this feeble form
    Did guide thee o'er the perilous deep—
Thy guardian angel through the storm,
    That did love's constant vigil keep.

Say not these tear-dimmed, sunken eyes
    Did cheer thee through the gloom of night—
Like' stars refulgent in the skies,
    Did shed o'er thee a heavenly light.

Say not that melancholy smile
    Did soothe thee o'er to placid rest,
And like an angel all the while,
    With golden wings did shield thy breast.

Say not this heart of throbbing dust
    Did prove to thee a solid rock,
Where thou didst firmly place thy trust
    When Death nigh dealt his fatal stroke

Say not thou lov'st me as thy life,
    That death alone shall thee estrange,
That I must be thy living life,
    For gold thou would'st not me exchange.

What though I wear a gifted name,
    Immortalised in history's page,
What though my brow is crowned with fame,
    Death wars within my bosom wage.

Through weary years of care and toil,
    Deep grief and thought have wrecked this form;
A death-shade round this bosom coils,
    That soon may feed the hungry worm

And it might wreck thy bosom's peace
    To link thy noble heart with mine,
Yet death alone would only cease
    My heart from yearning after thine.

And it might wrap thy soul in gloom,
    And cloud with care thy lofty brow,
And wed thee to a joyless doom,
    Would'st thou perform thy plighted vow.

Go, loving, trusting, faithful one,
    This image from thy soul remove;
O! strive this shattered heart to shun—
    It is not worthy of thy love.

Why would'st thou woo the blighting wind,
    And build thy castles up in air,
And dream of hope, then wake to find
    Their towers lie scattered in despair?

Why would'st thou pull the autumn rose,
    And wear it next thy loving heart,
And know that in its breast respose
    Death's deep consuming counterpart?

Why would'st thou to this shadow bow,
    To grasp a flower of phantom bloom,
And e'er its fragrance fanned thy brow,
    Behold it withered in ● tomb?

'Tis true that we have never met,
    Yet love like ours was seldom known;
And yet that love might bring regret
    When time had made me all thine own.

O! gaze upon this little carte,
    The emblem of thy promised wife,
And say could'st thou till death regard
    Her as the love-star of thy life.

Is she thy choice? Then take this hand,
    This heart thou prizest more than gold;
By Heaven's decree, by fate's command,
    The Factory Girl to thee is sold.

E. J., THE FACTORY GIRL.

CHAPELSHADE FACTORY, DUNDEE.

[POSTSCRIPT.]

O, hasten to thy fatherland!
    Thy God, who led thee o'er the main
In safety with his mighty hand,
    May bring thee safely back again.

Then I shall be thy happy bride;
    And when death's dark, all-sev'ring wave
Shall sweep me from thy faithful side,
    Thy tears, dear George, alone I crave.   E. J

To the Factory Girl.

SING on, fair empress of the gifted Nine,
    Chant forth thy soul-inspiring song of glee
Thy spotless brow doth still in beauty shine
    With fame's bright crown, so nobly won by thee.

Thy heaven-born music, so pure and unconfined,
    Has won thee a name that few possess—
Grace, innocence, and truth, and love combined,
    Abide within thy breast, sweet poetess.

Nature, sweet maiden, hath not me endowed
    With powers sufficient for to sing thy praise,
Yet one grand privilege she hath me allowed,
    Enchanting maiden—for to read thy lays.

When first within the Post thy lines did shine,
    Only from Heaven I thought such language came,
So touched with feeling and pure love divine;
    Full well dost thou deserve thy crown of fame.

Had I the gift of thee, or Edith fair,
  Oft would I sing in classic style to thee;
For with thy lays I nothing can compare,
  And nought on earth more sacred is to me.

And he whose breast doth wear thy trusting heart—
  Who sings of home and thee 'neath foreign skies—
May health and joy never from him depart,
  And fortune crown his youthful enterprise.

For though, dear Ellen, thou art left alone,
  With none save little Jasper for thy guide,
How happy wilt thou be when George comes home,
  To claim thee as his true and loving bride!

Adieu, sweet maid; may joy ne'er forsake thee,
  May grief nor sorrow never dim thine eyes;
When from thine earthly seat God's pleased to take thee,
  May one be vacant for thee in the skies.
                                        J. H. B. B.

To the Factory Girl.

Sweet Dundee girl, Old Scotia's muse
  With garlands crowns thy poet's brow;
The mantle of her Robert Burns,
  With golden folds, is round you now.
Thy bonnie verse, sae smooth and sweet,
  Has charmed my heart through to the core;
O, could I but thy face once meet,
  To tell a tale ne'er told before!

Were I the perfumed summer winds
  That 'mong the apple blossoms dwell,
I'd wander, blessed, far away
  To you, sweet poetess, Factory Girl,

And clasp thy lovely waist sae sma',
    Where grows the bonnie Scotch blue bell,
And pass a golden hour wi' her,
    The inspired angel, Factory Girl.

Alas! in vain, you golden dreams;
    Reflections grim the truth unfold;
Too late—no hope remains for me—
    The Factory Girl is gone—she's sold.
Thrice happy youth, re-cross the sea,
    And claim a prize more worth than gold;
The gods envy you in the sky,
    Your virtuous bride they all behold.

Sweet Dundee girl, a long adieu;
    Thy sparkling eyes, thy heart divine,
Thy ruby lips, like May's young rose,
    And angel form, can ne'er be mine.
When he who is thy heart's first choice
    With transport clasps thee to his breast,
May Cupid sportive round you fly,
    And angels guard their sister's rest.

GREENOCK, August 20, 1866.   D. NICOL.

To Scotia's Hard-Toiling Girl.

FAIR maiden, thy muse has awakened within me
    A rigid desire for to trace with my pen
The thoughts entertained when I found me at leisure,
    Soon after perusing thy sweet lyric gem.

Sweet bardess, sing on, thy lays are enchanting,
    And sweet are the notes they produce unto me;
Fair queen of old Scotia, thy songs they are flaunting
    From Clyde's bonnie banks to thy home in Dundee.

Thy image is seen in the wing that is forming
    The dews of the morning, that soon disappear
Before the bright sun, in its splendour adorning,
    And casting its rays saddened hearts for to cheer.

Thy voice has already sent pleasure among them
    Who have for long felt bitter grief and despair;
And the calm you've imparted to each laden bosom
    Is priceless, fair minstrel, and always doth cheer.

It lightens the burden that lies on the weary,
    And raises the victim that's bowed down in pain
With the cares of a world darksome and dreary,
    And leaves no desire on his part to remain.

But with you, dear Ellen—O! blessed be your station!
    May God, in His goodness, for ever watch o'er,
And protect the rare gift He's bestowed on a nation
    That welcomes thy produce right into the core!

Thy genius, bright gem, as the stars, is untarnished,
    And shines with a brilliancy equalled by none;
Thy fame it hath spread, and is yet still ascending—
    O! noble and great are the victories won.

Thus foremost, fair maiden, thy pen is thy weapon,
    Urged on to the conquest with judgment and skill;
And thy valuable works by men ever honoured,
    Have awakened up minds that were sullen and still.

O, calm be thy mind! may it ever find rest,
    And ne'er be disturbed or get cause for to whirl!
May the angels of bliss ever hover around you,
    And shield from all vice Scotia's hard-toiling girl!

'Tis sought for in prayer both evening and morning,
    All over the nation and far o'er the sea.
O, blest be that gifted one, Scotia adorning,
    Who strikes the sweet harp in our bonnie Dundee!

                      J. M'LATCHIE.

To the Factory Girl.

AWAKE, my muse, with all thy powers,
    I now must sing in hamely glee
One other strain to cheer the breast
    Of her who sings in sweet Dundee.
No world's care shall daunton me,
    Or stop me when I tune my lays;
For while I'm in a land that's free,
    I'll muse and sing to Ellen's praise.

Oft hath she lain on sorrow's bed,
    Without a friend to take her part;
Oft hath she sought the dark green shade—
    Alas! but with a trembling heart.
But now she shines bright as yon star
    Which sparkles in the evening sky;
Her name and fame have spread afar—
    Far as the fleet-winged dove can fly.

When summer comes back to our hills,
    And nature smiles on every tree,
Then I will stray where fancy fills
    My heart with love and liberty.
Then, Ellen, I will muse on thee
    When summer opes her every rose;
It surely can't be wrong in me
    To sing your praise where Calder flows.

Long may the genius of our land
    Attend you with her harmless smile;
Your much loved strains could charm the bard
    Who sung 'The Lass of Ballochmyle.'
Edith sings well, and proves to be
    Possessed with genius bright and grand;
But still she doth acknowledge thee
    The foremost of our musing band.

CALDERVALE.   DAVID MORRISON.

To the Poet.

My dear lack-a-daisy, I'm unco unaisy,
    Your verses I hae just been reading;
An' my word I will pass, you're no sic an' auld ass
    When rigg'd oot in a young poet's cleeding.

Your auld-farrant chiming an' Dorical rhyming
    Hae fairly brocht me to a stammer;
An' I dinna ken yet hoo my een hae been shut—
    They've surely been rubbit wi' glamour.

To think ye've got Hatty to be yer wee dawtie—
    Oh! wha in the warld would think it—
That ye thus could ensnare sic a wondrous fair,
    When yer pouchfu' o' bawbees ye clinkit?

Had ye sapeit and rubbit, or scrapit an' scrubbit
    For me as ye did for Miss Hatty,
I wad ne'er ta'en the flicht on yon eeriesome nicht
    That I near flegg'd the wits oot o' Watty.

But O! may guid guide us, and nae harm betide us!
    That nicht I ne'er will forget it;
For just like auld 'Cloot,' besmokit wi' soot,
    Awa frae the hoose-en' ye steppit.

Ye hinted an' taunted, ye girn'd an' ye gaunted,
    An' muttered yer auld lack-a-daisy;
Wi' yer auburn Jeans, an' yer new made preens,
    I thought ye had fairly gane crazy.

But listen, dear Kelly, awhile yet to Nelly—
    That sorrowfu', wofu', wild lassie:
Had ye drest like a clark, aye in a clean sark,
    I vow I wad ne'er been sae saucy;

For ye maun confess that a mad poetess,
    Aye soaring through dreamland's gay liftie,
Wad prefer a young man for her heart and her han'
    Before ane neither tastie nor tiftie.

An' noo, Maister Kelly, ye'll turn on puir Nelly,
    Because she did plumply refuse ye;
A hale nicht ye wad greet, then revenge ye wad seek,
    An' like a pick-pocket abuse me.

Ye are unco unhuman to frail, faithless woman—
    I only rejected yer proffer;
But there's naething sae crouse as a weel-washen louse,
    An' when Hatty accepted yer offer

On the banks o' the Lossie, sae verdant an' mossy,
    Ye'll brag o' her star-licht beauty;
O' her sweet begnet mou, an' her white magnet broo,
    That drew ye to gallant-man duty.

When beauty, I'm thinking, is won wi' the clinking
    O' mooly bawbees in auld breeches,
'Tis nae wonder, I ween, sic a fair angel queen
    Was bocht at the market o' riches.

But may ye be happy wi' hazel-ee'd Hatty,
    Wi' a hazel rung may ye ne'er peg her!
An' when ye get Hatty, then I will get Watty,
    Wha vows there is naething like leather!

He'll whistle an' sing like a mavis in spring,
    An' when I'm courting the Muses,
Wi' my auld rusty pens an' his rosetty ends,
    He'll cobble his boots an' his *Suses*.

An' though Fortune should spurn, yet we never should mourn,
    But wade through life's battle withoot her;
Contentment's the charm keeps a fond bosom warm—
    So I'll be content wi' my souter.

On oor honeymoon glee we'll sing o' Dundee—
    O' her braw factory lads an' young lasses;
An' may commerce an' steam lang be the bless'd theme
    O' her poets an' young poet-asses.

Since you an' yer Hatty, an' me an' my Watty,
    Ere lang will be twined in love's garlan',
Frae a heart that is true I wish much joy to you,
    Wi' yer dawty, an' me wi' my darlin'.

An' since I am bidden to come to yer weddin',
    Ye'll dance yer ainsel' wi' wee Nelly;
An' may your next address to oor daft poetess
    Be the birth o' a young poet Kelly.

E. J., THE FACTORY GIRL.

Lines to Edith,

WITH C. D. RUSSELL'S AND THE FACTORY GIRL'S CARTES.

O! tell me, sister Edith, if thou art a mortal born,
Or cam'st thou from the spirit land to cheer the all-forlorn;
To scatter fragrance of thy muse where weeds of grief have
    sprung,
And leave a lamp of hallow'd light where Care his clouds has
    flung?

Cam'st thou to pour a healing balm upon this bleeding heart,
And with thy sweet prophetic lays hope's solace to impart;
Foretelling brighter days to come, when I shall give my hand
To him that keeps my heart in troth, far in a foreign land?

Ah me! that such a heart as thine should e'er be wrung with
    woe—

That in a bosom saintly pure grief's rankling thorns should grow;
And disappointment's withering breath should blight thy form
    divine,
Or bitter gall o'erflow thy cup in place of life's bright wine.

Dear Edith, it is well for thee that fortune's on thy side,
Affliction's rod leans light on those whom wealth their wants
    provide;
But heavy doth it lie on them that's doomed their bread to win,
Fast working out their feeble life, alas! to keep it in.

'Tis not within the fragrant vale I gather summer flowers,
Nor is it in the garden fair I roam through dreamland bowers;
It is within the massive walls of factory dust and din
That I must woo my humble muse, her favour still to win.

'Tis not in lofty mansion hall love's lesson I must learn,
Nor yet a band of maidens fair fate wills me to govern;
It is the rude and ignorant whose insults I must brook,
The envious taunts of galling scorn and cold contemptuous look.

'Tis not by fair Madona's shrine I kneel in fervent prayer,
'Neath Gothic arch of painted glass, 'midst dazzling beauty rare;
It is amidst pestiferous oil that I inhale my breath,
'Midst pond'rous shafts revolving round the atmosphere of death.

Dear Edith, though corroding care may cloud that brow of thine,
Yet happy, happy is thy lot; 'tis Heaven's compar'd with mine!
Could'st thou but see the Factory Girl when bending o'er her
    loom,
Or could thou but escort her home to her cold cheerless room,

Where no one, save my faithful cat, awaits my coming home,
And whilst I light my fireless grate it sings a welcome song,
And then it climbeth on my breast and gazeth in my face—
The very nature of my mood within mine eyes to trace.

And if perchance I heed it not, then will it break the spell
And all the anguish of its heart in its own language tell;

Often hath it lapped the tear that did my cheeks imbue—
It would be well for many men their hearts were half as true.

Then, sister, such as thou and I would have no cause to mourn;
Nor blighted love nor bitter wrongs in woman's bosom burn;
Nor loved ones wander at their will to cast our love away,
But make our hearts their Mammon shrine, love's homage there to pay.

Sister, where's the bright-eyed youth who coldly left thy side,
When duty-bound thou didst obey the dictates of thy pride?
Is there no hope-star left to light the lonely wanderer's track?
No mystic charm to woo and win the loved, the lost one, back?

Surely he knoweth not thy worth, the charm thou canst impart—
The witching spell which thou canst fling around thy nation's heart—
Or soon he would return again from lands far o'er the sea,
And in the rose-leaved valley fair re-pledge his love to thee.

Dear Edith, if he was a prince—nay, more, a royal king—
Proud might he be down at thy feet his jewell'd crown to fling;
Proud might he be to gain thy heart, as proud to win thy hand,
For thine is worth a kingdom's wealth hath no power to command.

Forgive me, sister Edith, if perchance I may forget,
And ope the flood-gates of the heart—the fountains of regret—
Recalling joys that may perchance be dead for evermore.
But stay—the love thou lack'st on earth thou'lt find on heavenly shore.

One moment yet, my sister dear, before I say adieu—
This earth seems heaven to linger thus with one so good and true.
All I can give thee as a gift to prove my love unknown;
Accept the *carte* of my betrothed, accompanied with my own.

E. J., THE FACTORY GIRL.

Lines by Edith,
ON RECEIVING THE CARTES OF MR RUSSELL AND THE FACTORY GIRL.

Not many moons have waned since, from yon distant factory wall,
A measure strange and sweet did on our wild'ring senses fall,
And still the strain is sounding on, though mellower in its flow,
And rising richer o'er the din that jars that world below.

' That strain again—it had a dying fall '—altho' not borne
By sweet south o'er a violet bank, but from thy hearth forlorn,
Sweet sister, for the strain was thine; and, maiden, would'st thou know
That thou wak'st in me a love that more and more doth grow.

Sister, some strange and witching spell thy spirit casts o'er mine,
It lights the dull grey eye of day, and o'er my dreams doth shine;
With lamp in hand, I saw thee by my bed the other night,
And thou wert beck'ning me to some new mission in its light.

I knew thee then but through thy minstrelsy, as spirit rare,
Clad in a robe of gossamer—a creature of the air ;
But from my mantel-shelf to-night a form is looking down—
Is this thy face, fair girl, thy braided hair, thy flowing gown?

If this be thee, why hath the rose-bloom faded from thy cheek?
And why in that sad sunken eye seek we, but vainly seek,
The laughing-child that twined the daisy-chain on Glasgow Green,
And chose, at jing-a-ring, young Colin from the ranks between ?

And, lady, dost thou ask where fled the bloom that marked her then ?
See'st thou yon factory wall, so dingy and so grim ?' Ah, when
Thou'st entered there, that fume of horrid oil, that stifling air,
And deafening din of many wheels, will quickly tell thee where.

O, sister, did yon gaudy crowd thy virtues love like me,
Not longer in the factory gloom should'st thou entombed be;
Not longer should'st thou come at eve to thy chill, cheerless
    room,
With fireless grate, and but the old cat crouching in the gloom.

A spot is burning on my country's brow that sunny lands
Have smiled upon; she's built the poet's tomb with willing hands;
While scarce a gift, a smile of hers did bless his living fate,
A spot burns on his stone, and winds and echoes wail 'Too late.'

But, sister, from another point I'd read thy face to-night,
For in that deep, sad eye of thine I see a fount of light,
That sorrow may not quench, whose burning beam hath burst
    afar,
And o'er the world its gems is casting now like meteor star.

Yet who to carte-board cold can ere confine a poet's face?
And where the art or artist who, at passing glance, can trace
Those wavy lines of light and shade that genius flings around,
As shadows pass from summer grass upon the wild flowers
    mound?

And who is this, my sister sweet, that's seated by thy side?
I like that pensive face, that drooping eye, that seems to hide
Some fair, fair world of hopes and dreams deep from the night
    wind's scorn—
Music that's made for solitude, like note of summer morn.

It seems as if this traveller and I had climb'd life's steep
Wrapt in reserve, till thy brave song burst o'er the waters deep,
And threw o'er me the minstrel robe I ne'er had hoped to wear,
And made me come before the world to tell thy talents rare.

And him it drew, a lover, to thy side, who's found at last
The dream-maid of his muse; and soon those dreary waters past,

That darkly flow 'twixt him and thee; he'll scatter o'er thy
    brow
The pale white orange flowers, with poet wreath that decks it
    now.

Ah, sister! had I been a youth, this tale would have been mine;
I'd whispered in thine ear such vows while beat my heart by
    thine.
Before this deeper love of thine will sister love grow cold?
Still take my heart that was another's—through life I'll thee
    enfold.

Farewell, my noble sister; thou'st had strength to do and dare,
And rise 'bove vulgar scorn; thy meed of merit thou wilt wear.
This *carte* of thine I'll carry in my bosom night and day,
And when I lingering lag 'Excelsior' 'twill seem to say.

                                        EDITH.

Lines to Mr Daniel Syme, Lanark.

WHILST other minstrels' harps are heard
    To sing their kindred spirits' praise,
Shall I forget the Lanark bard,
    Who long since cheer'd me with his lays?

Shall I forget thee, Daniel Syme,
    Who sung in sweet spring time to me
Of joys I yet would share with him
    Whose bride alone I've vow'd to be?

No, sooner shall the birds forget
    To build their nests upon the tree;
Sooner the sun shall cease to set
    In western sky far o'er the sea;

Sooner shall flowerets cease to grow,
    The vaults of heaven for age be dim,
The ocean cease to ebb and flow,
    Ere I forget thee, Daniel Syme.

My cares may throw thee in the shade,
    But never can thy name efface;
Thy noble worth can never fade,
    Nor in this bosom lose its place.

Thy name is written in my heart,
    My album doth enclose thy *carte;*
Until death tears life's links apart
    I'll mark thee with a friend's regard.

The verses on thy 'baby boy'
    Hang on my lonely chamber walls,
Not as an ornamental toy,
    But as a gift that still enthrals

My soul with grief, and fills mine eyes
    With tears, but rarely seen to flow,
Save from a heart doth sympathise
    With love that none save parents know.

Weep not, dear friends, o'er thy first-born—
    Oh! what avail thy tears or sighs?
Thy angel gem, without a thorn,
    Blooms in a bower beyond the skies.

This humble lay which I have penned
    May unto thee this truth unfurl:
That thou art still the much-loved friend
    Of Dundee's lowly Factory Girl.

                      E. J.

Lines to Ellen, the Factory Girl.

DEAR ELLEN, when you read these lines, O, throw them not aside!
O, do not laugh at them in scorn, or turn away in pride!
I know 'tis a presumptuous thought for me to thee to write,
For, Ellen, feeble are the words that my pen can indite.

Had fortune smiled upon thy birth and favoured thee with wealth,
Then, Ellen, I would be content with praying for your health;
But since I know that you, like me, are forced your bread to win,
Exposed to many dangers 'mid the factory's smoke and din,

I know you have a feeling heart—that you will not be stern,
Nor deem it curiosity your history to learn;
Although I never saw thy face, yet I have read thy lays,
And 'tis my earnest prayer for thee that thou'lt see many days.

A year ago this very month I read your touching song—
Your last farewell to your betrothed, just after he had gone;
My thoughts were with you ever since—I thought of writing then,
But courage I could not call forth, and fear held back my pen.

Hast thou no mother, Ellen dear, to know thy griefs and fears,
No sister who hath shared thy joys through all thy childish years,
No brother's merry coaxing ways to welcome thee at home,
No father dear, in his arm-chair—are all those loved ones gone?

I know your heart is sensitive, and that you ill can brook
The sneer from those you work beside, the cold contemptuous look;
Tho' I have met with some of those, the number is but few—
The most of those I work beside are friends sincere and true.

I rise each morn at six o'clock, and pray that God will guide
Me through the duties of the day, whatever ill betide;

And when at night I lay me down, in calm and quiet repose,
I sleep the dreamless sleep of health contentment only knows.

For, dearest, in this world, you know, the sun's not always shining,
But underneath each heavy cloud there lies a silver lining;
Although thou art companionless, with no friend save thy cat,
I trust 'twill not be so with thee when thy betrothed comes back.

Thine eyes with love shall sparkling beam when he comes back again
To claim the hand thou promised him before he crossed the main;
Then I will wake my feeble muse, and let my song be heard,
A marriage sonnet unto him—St Ninian's noble bard.

GLASGOW, Nov. 21, 1866.　　　　　　　　　　　ISABEL.

Lines to Isabel from the Factory Girl.

DEAR ISABEL, the star of night is gleaming
　　All through the casement of my lonely room,
Whilst from my lowly couch of thee I'm dreaming,
　　Wrapt in the curtains of night's sable gloom.

I'm all alone, save with my little Jesper—
　　That's ever faithful, ever true to me;
As cloister'd nun doth sing at evening vesper,
　　So doth my pet one chaunt its song of glee.

Hush'd now its song, and silence is pervading
　　The weary world, that dreams in calm repose;
Now thy sweet muse my languid soul doth laden,
　　As dew-drops hail the summer morning's rose.

Dear Isabel, methinks I hear thee singing—
  Thy plaintive strain my soul's deep fount doth stir;
The well-stream of my heart with love is springing,
  And joy breaks forth from sorrow's sepulchre.

Dear Isabel, thou fain wouldst learn my history—
  Couldst thou feel joy to learn a tale of woe
That's linked with many a strange and cruel mystery,
  Which God in Heaven alone can ever know?

I leave my wrongs with Him—He will avenge them—
  In His almighty wisdom to destroy;
And those that wronged me I will ne'er estrange them;
  Theirs may be grief perchance when mine is joy.

No hatred in my heart I ever cherish'd;
  When open to conviction, they shall see
The golden dreams that in my bosom perished
  Beneath the falsehoods which they heaped on me.

My life's young years were spent in dark repining,
  In persecution, falsehood, and envy;
But now a world of love is round me twining—
  My fame is soaring upwards to the sky.

Now, tell me, Isabel, where I may find thee,
  From whence thou cam'st, and who, and what thou art?
For like my sister Edith thou dost bind me
  With chords of melody around my heart.

And tell me dost thou know my sister Edith?
  Hast thou e'er heard or read her mystic lays?
Her love-born muse my thirsting soul still feedeth
  With glowing light of Heaven's celestial rays.

And tell me, songstress of St Mungo's city,
    What marvellous charm the world finds in me;
Is it my murmuring songs—my love-lorn ditty,
    Still fraught with sighs and tears of misery?

Is it because I have no gentle mother
    To kiss away the sad unbidden tear—
No loving sister, no fond laughing brother,
    No doating father this lone heart to cheer?

Is it because I am an orphan lonely
    A thousand hearts doth sympathise with me,
And countless lovers vow to love me only,
    Would I forsake him far across the sea?

Dear Isabel, the vows that I have spoken,
    The pledge I gave his bride alone to be,
By his own will perchance may yet be broken,
    But ne'er in life shall they be broke by me.

Should he return and wish to wed another
    More like himself—all handsome, young, and fair,
Then I shall love him as I would a brother—
    A sister's love from me he'll ever share.

And when thou sing'st to him his marriage sonnet
    (St Ninian's bard that thou dost wish so well),
Then I shall breathe a prayer of love upon it,
    And bless thee ever, gentle Isabel.

Lines to Mr David Morrison, Caldervale.

EARTH'S glorious Day-King to his slumber has gone,
And the fair Queen of Night hath ascended her throne;
And the bright stars are beaming all radiant now,
Like a cor'net of glory encircling her brow.

The hired sons of toil, with their labour opprest,
Unconscious of care, are now slumbering at rest,
Whilst Ellen is wandering the night winds among,
She is wooing her sad muse and sighing its song.

Ah! blow gently ye breezes of night's silent hour,
When shades of the dead are invested with power;
Sweet Spirit of Genius that floats on the gale,
O fly fast to the loved bard of fair Caldervale!

And tell him his love-melting muse I have heard,
Far more sweet than the lay of a Paradise bird;
Like the song of a seraph 'twas wafted to me
On the gold wings of August to bonnie Dundee.

Tell it came ere the blast of September's chill breath
Had scattered the wan leaves like heralds of death,
Ere trees lost their foilage and flowers their rich bloom,
Or the glad face of nature was shaded with gloom.

Tell it came when the reapers' sweet song of the morn
Did blend with the warblers that sung from the thorn,
Whilst the 'Harvest Queen' gathered her rich golden grain,
And stripped nature's mantle from valley and plain.

Tell it came when this bosom was bursting with grief,
But its melody poured the sweet balm of relief
On this sad heart, that drank up the love-melting tale,
As it blessed the dear bard of fair Caldervale.

Haste, and tell him to weep not for Maggie that's dead,
For her pure, spotless spirit to Heaven hath fled;
The Saviour hath gathered the lamb in His fold,
And crowned her with glory far brighter than gold.

Though he ne'er will behold her again on this earth,
Nor her sweet gentle kiss swell his bosom with mirth;
Yet 'tis joy for to know that she sorrows no more,
But she sings a glad angel on Heaven's bright shore.

And O! tell him to sing his sweet soul-stirring strains,
To gladden grief's woes and to lighten life's chains;
That love songs like his a sweet solace can bring
To the desolate bosom that's felt sorrow's sting.

And O! tell him to sing of our Hogg and our Burns,
Of our dear Tannahill, whom a nation now mourns,
That the people of Paisley will not raise a stone
As a token of love for their bard, ever gone.

But though never a stone nor a statue should stand
To mark his loved memory on old Scotland's strand,
Our dear Tannahill still remembered shall be
Whilst the birds build their nests on fair Craigielea.

And tell him to sing of the famed ploughman's wife
Who hath nobly fought in sweet minstrelsy's strife;
Whose harp hath awoke the long slumbering regard
Which wrapt in oblivion the worth of that bard.

Ah! my frail harp's too weak of her merits to sing,
Or a halo of honour around her to fling;
O! had I but the wealth of some miser, untold,
I would weave her dear name in a garland of gold.

And O! tell him to sing of his joys and his woes,
In the still hour of night where sweet Calder stream flows;
That my spirit shall linger and listen his song
Whilst he wanders the moonbeams and night shades among.

And let Faith be his helmet, his pen be his sword,
And let Truth be his shield, and Love his watchword;
Let Hope be his standard, and Heaven his right;
Let the Muse be the field whereon he doth fight.

If Dundee's Factory Girl he would fain imitate,
Then a warrior minstrel he must personate;
And his banner of fame unfurled will be
Far higher than Ellen's of bonnie Dundee.

Sweet Spirit of Genius, go tell him all this,
And impress on his brow a pure holy kiss;
Ere you bid him farewell, present him this *carte*,
As a token from me to Caldervale's bard.

SONGS.

The Lad of Burnbank Mill.

I HAVE loved thee as a brother,
   With love true and sincere,
And I ne'er can love another
   With love so true and dear.
I have borne with silent sadness
   Each rival foe's ill-will;
Ah! my heart's bereaved of gladness
   For the Lad of Burnbank Mill.

Whilst around me foes are scorning,
   The tears they dim mine eyes;
With a smile my lips adorning,
   I repel my bosom's sighs,
And I tell them that I love thee,
   And that I ever will;
Ah! I prize none else above thee,
   Sweet Lad of Burnbank Mill.

Like the lilies by yon fountain
   That smiles unto the sun,
And like daisies on the mountain
   Is that lad my heart has won;
And more sweet than dew adorning
   The snow-drop on the hill,
Sweet as roses blown in morning
   Is the Lad of Burnbank Mill.

Broken Vows.

Oh tell me not my cheeks are faded,
    That sorrow clouds my brow;
Nor say my once bright eyes are shaded
    From every pleasure now.

Oh tell me not my wasting form
    Is hastening to decay;
Nor say my joys of youth's bright morn
    Have lasted but a day.

Oh tell me not yon silent grave
    Is yawning to receive me;
Nor say I dread lest death's dark wave
    Upon its ocean heave me.

Oh tell me not, for well I know
    My heart, that burns with anguish,
From grief and care will soon beat low,
    And cease to love and languish.

Oh tell me not, when I am dead,
    The vows that he hath spoken
Shall rush like waters o'er his head,
    His heart, like mine, be broken.

Bogie and I.

O there ne'er was a lassie that e'er lo'ed a laddie,
    But she in that laddie saw some secret wile;
If his form wasna fair, nor yet winsome and gawdie,
    He had something sweeter—a charm in his smile.

O I hae a laddie that is dear, dear unto me,
    And nane kens how oft for that laddie I sigh;
O there's nae tongue can tell how weel I lo'e young Jamie,
    When he looks in my face saying—Bogle and I.

O how sweet is the smile that has wiled my heart frae me,
    And nae star o' hope can my bosom descry;
Yet, far dearer than life's-light tae me is my Jamie,
    When he looks in my face saying—Bogle and I.

And he told me yestreen as we baith sat thegither,
    That they had been comrades for years lang gane by;
O believe me, I lo'e him as weel as a brither,
    For there ne'er were twa comrades like Bogle and I.

O wherever I gang he's aye willin' tae gane till,
    And aught that I wish for he'll never deny;
And what promise he mak's he's aye sure tae stan' till;
    There ne'er were twa comrades like Bogle and I.

I watched that dear laddie while thus he was speaking,
    His dark hazel een shone like stars in the sky,
And his smile, bright as sunshine, set my heart abeating
    When he looked in my face saying—Bogle and I.

O there ne'er were three words by a mortal e'er spoken
    That e'er rent a bosom wi' love's secret sigh;
O there ne'er was a smile left a heart nearly broken,
    As young Jamie's left mine saying—Bogle and I.

O they are the words that through life shall endear me,
    Whate'er be my fate till death's dark hour is nigh;
Through sunshine and shadow his form will be near me,
    Still soothing my sad soul with Bogle and I.

We've Parted.

We've parted, but thy name shall be
　　The banner of my life,
Unfurled still to wave o'er thee
　　'Midst falsehood's galling strife.
The phantom of thy youthful form
　　Shall haunt me evermore,
Like rosebud opening to the morn,
　　Whilst I thy loss deplore.

We've parted—Heavens! thus to part,
　　The hope of future years,
The chosen loved one of my heart,
　　That melteth now in tears.
Thy very shadow made me bow,
　　I've knelt thy form before,
And listened to thy first love vow;
　　Now I thy loss deplore.

We've parted, like a poor outcast
　　I pass my time alone;
A retrospect left of the past
　　Is all that I can own.
Thy deep deceit, thy faithless heart,
　　My memory rushes o'er,
And stings my soul with sorrow's dart
　　Whilst I thy loss deplore.

We've parted, but thou'rt ever mine
　　By promise, pledge, and vow;
Thou canst not kneel before Love's shrine
　　To wed another now.

  Yes, Jamie, thou'rt ever mine,
   Though thou canst ne'er restore
  The heart I gave in change for thine—
   Farewell for evermore.

My Childhood's Hours.

O BRING me again the sweet days of my childhood,
 Those bright blessed hours of innocent glee,
When I roamed Glasgow Green and Cathkin's green wildwood,
 Gathering May flowers and chasing the bee.

Gleaning the wheat fields, climbing the mountain,
 Startling the linnet that sang in the glen,
Washing my doll's face at Arn's Well fountain—
 O! who would not wish back the joys I had then,

When catching the butterfly while it was sucking
 Sweet dew from the pale rose that sprung on the lea,
And wreathing the wild flowers till sunbeams were setting
 Far in the west o'er the dark, wide, blue sea;

Gaily dancing and singing, a light-hearted girl,
 Ne'er dreaming then that love could decoy;
Wildly tossing my head with its bright sunny curls,
 And placing upon it the cap of some boy.

Ah! how my light blue eyes with joy then were beaming!
 Care o'er my bosom his clouds had not flung,
And hope round my heart was like young starlights gleaming,
 Whilst with my playmates so sweetly I sung.

Yea, those were the days of my life's purest pleasure,
 When love was an infant, budding to bloom;
I dreamed not that fate would soon shorten their measure,
 And darken their sunshine with shadows of gloom.

But where are those days, now, of innocent gladness?
    Oh! tell me, cruel Fate, the cause of this change;
And why are those pleasures grown sorrow and sadness?
    Hearts that were kind then are now cold and strange.

Farewell for ever, sweet scenes of my childhood,
    When young lovers loved me, with true hearts they smiled;
No more shall I wander through Cathkin's green wildwood,
    Nor feel e'er I die as I felt when a child.

The Young Man's Darling.

A CRAZY auld man whiles comes frae Lochee,
    An' he ca's me prood an' haughty;
O! lack-a-daisy, he is coorting me,
    An' wants me to be his dawtie.
He brags o' his gear an' boasts o' his lan',
    An' wonders hoo I'm sae naughty
As no tae gie him my heart an' han',
    An' be his bonnie wee dawtie.
    But I'll be a young man's darling
        Though humble be my cell;
    I'll ne'er be the auld man's dawtie
        While I am bonnie Nell.

A cankered carl, the emblem o' death,
    Could ne'er warm my heart wi' pleasure;
His frosty frown an' his wintry breath
    Would tarnish his gowden treasure.
What tho' he would dress me gay as a queen,
    Mammon's gold sceptre swirling,
When lost for aye would be Love's young dream—
    Na, I'll be a young man's darling.

O! I'll be a young man's darling,
  Tho' fate blaws keen an' snell;
I'll ne'er be the auld man's dawtie
  While I am bonnie Nell.

O! lack-a-daisy, his dark ingle side
  Is sair in want o' a starling;
Young Peg or Jean he may choose for a bride,
  For I'll be a young man's darling.
Let Hatty or Isa, whae'er they may be,
  Send his auld hundreds whirling,
For had he a million, he'll ne'er get me,
  For I'll be a young man's darling.
O! I'll be a young man's darling,
  His bonnie Nell I'll be;
What needs the carl be harling
  Awa' frae his hive in Lochee?

A Voice from the Mountains.

A RUMOUR is pealing through castle and shealing—
  Like the shock of an earthquake it soundeth afar—
That Napoleon is coming, his eagles he's pluming,
  To soar through our land on the pinions of war.
But never—no, never, whilst Clutha's famed river
  Doth pour out her pure soul to the wide boundless sea,
Shall Frenchmen invade us like cowards degraded,
  For our land is the home of the brave and the free.

  Riflemen, riflemen, heroes of glory,
    We'll come from the mountains, the valley, and glen,
  Our names to enrol in fame's golden story,
    And join in your ranks, ye brave riflemen.

The red field ot Flodden, the moor of Culloden,
    And Bannockburn's victory her bosom inspires,
For valour still weepeth o'er heroes that sleepeth,
    Since her freedom was bought with the blood of our sires.
The flock-bleating mountain, the rock-leaping fountain,
    The feather-winged warbler and wild busy bee,
Where thistle and heather both twine up together,
    Re-echo the song of the brave and the free.

    Riflemen, riflemen, heroes of glory, &c.

Through Britain's vast nations and her loftiest stations,
    Her banners of glory shall ever wave free;
No foe shall estrange her, no despot avenge her—
    None shall crush her beneath a vile dastard decree.
Whilst her bold mountaineers can be trained Volunteers,
    Old England's fair Queen need not dream of dismay;
From mountain and valley her armies shall ally,
    And the eagles become her proud lion's prey.

    Riflemen, riflemen, heroes of glory,
        We'll come from the mountains, the valley, and glen,
    To conquer or die for the loved land of story,
        The home of the freeman and brave riflemen.

O! Scotland, my Country.

WRITTEN IN BELFAST, APRIL, 1857.

O! SCOTLAND, my country, thou land of my father,
    When shall I gaze on thy heath hills again?
O! when shall I see the sweet calm twilight gather
    Amang the grey cairns of my auld native hame?

For thou art the dear land where freedom's bells blossom,
    Thy glens are the martyrs and patriots' graves,
And bright is the glory that beams in thy bosom,
    And green are the fields where thy proud thistle waves.

    O! Scotland, my country, wherever I wander,
        Thy name to my bosom a guide star shall be;
    On the deeds of thy Wallace often I'll ponder,
        Wha focht and wha fell, my country, for thee.

Dear land of my kindred, wha wadna adore thee,
    That e'er heard thy history of heroes so brave?
Sweet home of the freeman, there never hung o'er thee
    The curse of a tyrant nor tear of a slave.
The usurping Southron long tried thy undoing,
    Thy Wallace he conquered, though basely he fell,
And auld Bothwell Castle, that moulders in ruin,
    Whilst ivy clings roond it his valour shall tell.

    O! Scotland, my country, wherever I wander, &c.

Let proud England boast of her high titled gentry,
    Her queens and her princes, her palace and throne;
Despite a' her grandeur, she'll ne'er be a country
    Emblazon'd wi' fame like my auld Caledon.
Let green Erin boast of her wild woven bowers,
    Her ivy-clad walls and her green shamrock soil;
The spirit of bigotry springs wi' her flowers
    A feeling of discord inhabits her isle.

    O! Scotland, my country, wherever I wander, &c.

A change hath passed o'er thee; sad, sad is the story
    That brings the saut tears of grief fast frae my e'e;
They tell me thy heath hills look dismal and hoary,
    Hung round wi' the curtains of dark poverty.

O ! Scotland, my country, my forefathers' nation,
  My heart bleeds to hear of thy sorrow and pain ;
To deem thy brave sons grow weak wi' starvation,
  O, God, that they had but their Wallace again !

    O ! Scotland, my country, wherever I wander,
      My heart's purest wish still shall linger wi' thee ;
    On the deeds of thy Wallace I often ponder,
      And wish, for thy sake, I a Wallace could be.

A Song of War.
WRITTEN IN BELFAST, OCTOBER, 1857.

Tune—'JEANETTE AND JEANOT.'

YE working men of Britain, I will sing to you a song,
And if you are not pleased with it, I hope you'll pass along,
For I'm not inclined to quarrel nor see you fight or spar,
You'll hear, from what I've got to say, I am not fond of war,
You'll hear, from what I've got to say, I am not fond of war.

The golden spires of learning are towering in their height,
And men are so enlighten'd now, they know the wrong from
  right.
When art and science have excelled, and shining like a star,
Shall the people of the present age be trampled down by war ?
Shall the people of the present age be trampled down by war ?

What is our House of Lords about—our men of Parliament ?
They waste their time in passing bills small trifles to prevent ;
Let them look at the starving poor—it would be better far
If they would pass a bill for peace, and end this fatal war,
If they would pass a bill for peace, and end this fatal war.

Our kingdoms three are lying waste by rebels of the Crown,
O, for ten thousand Wallace wights to rise and pull them down!
I thought that Britain would have peace when she conquer'd
    the Czar,
But we have another Nicholas lying wait for war,
But we have another Nicholas lying wait for war.

It is the war that has brought on this dismal want and woe,
It is the poor man pays for all, and that you all do know,
For pale-faced Famine enters in his cabin door to bar,
And shuts out life's gay sunshine, then with hunger he must war,
And shuts out life's gay sunshine, then with hunger he must war.

Yet, strange to say, if our poor men would quarrel for their right,
Some of our prison magistrates would pay them for their fight;
But if an emperor or king gets ought his peace to mar,
He can never end his quarrels without a horrid war,
He can never end his quarrels without a horrid war.

I wish I had lived in the days of noble Joan of Arc,
Although I am not fond of war, I have a daring heart,
And to defend the working man the lordling I would dare,
For if we had less foreign lords, then we would have less war,
For if we had less foreign lords, then we would have less war.

Now, ye working men of Britain, in this dark dismal hour,
If you must fight, let it be right that sways you in its power,
And show that right shall conquer might, despite of crown or star.
Down with those foreign despots that are starving us with war!
Down with those foreign despots that are starving us with war!

My Maggie.
A SONG WRITTEN BY THE REQUEST OF AN ADMIRER.

O! FAR may ye roam through the glen, o'er the mountain,
    Aroond the Law Hill an' awa' by Lochee;
And far may ye wander by Logie's clear fountain—
    A lass like my Maggie, O whaur will ye ?
She's aye sweetly smiling, my puir heart beguiling,
    Her red rosy cheeks an' her bonnie blue e'e;
So gentle her nature, so comely her feature,
    A lass like my Maggie there's no in Dundee.

Oft I've been courting and oft I've been sporting,
    And young sweethearts I've had of every degree;
But nane can come forward tae match Maggie Dorward,
    O! she is the love-star that beams bricht on me.
And oft I've been roaming alane in the gloaming,
    Whar lads and young lasses were sporting wi' glee;
And sae blythely I've sang until Rosebank Ha's rang—
    A lass like my Maggie there's no in Dundee.

When winter's reposing, and summer's disclosing
    Her primrose and lily on ilka green lea,
The dew in the morning the rosebud adorning,
    Mair pure than my Maggie it cannot be.
When autumn comes mellow, wi' corn waving yellow,
    And the rich golden foliage drapes every tree,
Oor vows shall be plighted, oor hearts be united,
    And my bonnie Maggie my wifie shall be.

The Miller Lad.

O, WEEL I lo'e the miller lad that stands at yonder gate,
My heart is sair and unco sad wi' sighing o'er my fate;
His bonnie face within my breast has ta'en up its abode—
O weel I lo'e the miller lad that's in Commercial Road.

His rosy cheeks and star-light een they gie such joy to me,
I wouldna gie ae glance o' them for treasures out the sea;
Nae world's gear would grieve my heart, nae wealth e'er be my god,
Could I but win the miller lad that's in Commercial Road.

O could I win that laddie's heart, his love nae mair tae tine,
But lock it up within my ain, and it would aye be mine;
And late an' early would I toil to keep him braw and snod,
For weel I lo'e the miller lad that's in Commercial Road.

I canna see a lad sae sweet in a' Hutchesontoon,
And mony braw anes I could see if I would jist gang roon',
Till I come tae M'Lellan's gate, that is baith big and broad,
But nane can match the miller lad that's in Commercial Road.

Oh sair, alas! I rue the day that laddie's face I saw,
For oh I feel his winning smile has wiled my heart awa';
I sit me doon on Clutha's bank, upon the dewy sod,
Tae muse upon the miller lad that's in Commercial Road.

But oh that bonnie laddie's love frae me lies far awa',
It is a dark and thorny path that comes between us twa,
For oh I wear a blighted heart, borne doon wi' sorrow's load,
I ne'er can win the miller lad that's in Commercial Road.

The Nicht I Married Tom.

Tune—'JOHN ANDERSON, MY JO JOHN.'

THE nicht I went to marry Tom I hadna ae bawbee,
An' if I like to tell the truth, the deil o' ane had he;
Yet had I got my choice, atweel, o' kingdom or gay throne,
I wadna changed my mind, I vow, the nicht I married Tom.

An' we hadna bed nor blanket, nor had we hoose or hame,
And when we baith got buckled fast, an' frae the parson's came,

Like dizzy geese amang the snaw thro' ilk street we did roam,
Yet earth it seemed a heaven tae me the nicht I married Tom.

He was a sawyer tae his trade, an' times were unco dull,
He had been idle for a month, tho' wood was in the mill,
His master had nae orders an' he bade the men begone,
So without siller, hoose, or wark, the nicht I married Tom.

The hoose whar I was lodging in it was baith big and bien;
I asked the mistress if she'd let us baith sleep there at e'en?
She answered, Ye are welcome, and in a friendly tone
She said, I will dae mair than that since you have married Tom.

She made for us a cup o' tea, and aff tae bed we went;
Tho' poverty hung o'er oor heads, love made us baith content,
His fond embrace, the kindly kiss he laid my lips upon,
Made me forget my plackless purse the nicht I married Tom,

Tom soon got wark, and sae did I; wi' love and anxious care
We got as much as did oor turn, and syne we gathered mair.
An' noo we hae a gude fu' hoose, wi' plenty in an' on—
As yet I ne'er had cause tae rue the nicht I married Tom.

The Thistle Hall.*

Tune—'KELVIN GROVE.'

O! YOU'RE welcome, sons of toil, to the Thistle Hall,
Where the flowers of freedom smile in the Thistle Hall;

* This song was sung by the authoress in the Thistle Hall, on the 7th February, 1866, in commemoration of Mr James Dorward, powerloom manager, being presented with a handsome sofa, as a token of gratitude and respect, from the workers under his charge in the powerloom department, Chapelshade Works, Dundee.

The like I ne'er did see since I came unto Dundee—
O! each face smiles sweet wi' glee in the Thistle Hall.

O! there's lasses sweet and fair in the Thistle Hall,
A' dressed so neat and rare in the Thistle Hall;
Wi' ribbons pink and blue, wi' Garibaldies too,
And wi' cheeks of rosy hue in the Thistle Hall.

O! there's lads frae east and west in the Thistle Hall,
Like gentlemen they're dressed in the Thistle Hall;
They bring honour and renown to our bonnie Dundee town,
That shall yet be handed down from the Thistle Hall.

O! there's managers and men in the Thistle Hall,
And a foreman, tae, I ken, in the Thistle Hall,
That ne'er will blush wi' shame to read his honoured name
In the records of our fame in the Thistle Hall.

O! we are nae met for fame in the Thistle Hall,
'Tis friendship is our aim in the Thistle Hall,
To give honour where it's due to our foreman just and true,
And this night we ne'er shall rue in the Thistle Hall.

O! we have a token here in the Thistle Hall,
'Tis a gift of love sincere in the Thistle Hall;
Tho' the night is but a span, yet we'll do the best we can,
All to honour our foreman in the Thistle Hall.

O! then, here's to his dear wife in the Thistle Hall,
She's the guide-star of his life in the Thistle Hall,
And his family, ane and a', sae bonnie, trig, and braw,
May no harm o'er them befa' in the Thistle Hall.

O! then heart and hand agree in the Thistle Hall,
And still let our watchword be in the Thistle Hall,
That we long may earn our bread in the bonnie Chapelshade,
By his foremanship still led near the Thistle Hall.

Then with love and unity in the Thistle Hall,
Give James Dorward three-times-three in the Thistle Hall;
Whilst the Chapelshade doth flourish our union still we'll nourish,
And true worth we still shall cherish in the Thistle Hall.

Lord Raglan's Address to the Allied Armies.

Tune—'KATHLEEN MAVOURNEEN.'

HARK! my brave soldiers, the trumpet is sounding,
    The banners are borne on the peril of life;
See how the Cossacks like cowards are bounding
    Away from the field of carnage and strife.
Let not the visions of home and friends haunt you,
    To do or to die is the motto we have;
Let not the groans of the dying e'er daunt you,
    Sebastopol's ours—a prize or a grave.
    Then on to the field, ye brave sons of glory,
        On to the field where the banners wave high;
    Your names are enrolled in fame's golden story—
        Fight for Sebastopol, conquer or die.

There's many a brave man has fallen before you—
    His friends and his country he'll never see more;
And if you should fall, your friends will deplore you
    When laurels of honour shall spring from your gore.
Love will dream o'er you which cannot defend you,
    Or watch o'er the danger that threatens your life;
Hearts will deplore you that cannot attend you,
    When death lays you low on the red field of strife.
    Then on to the field, ye brave sons of glory, &c.

Onward! my heroes—a reward doth await you,
　　For Raglan shall never let bravery be lost;
Onward! let nothing but death e'er defeat you—
　　Let yours be the honour, the glory, the boast.
Your orphans and widows shall all be provided
　　　　With food and with raiment if you should be slain,
And each faithful sweetheart be guarded and guided
　　If her gallant lover returns not again.
　　　　Then on to the field, ye brave sons of glory, &c.

Do you not deem the scene will be galling
　　To Menschikoff while he stands gazing around?
There's ten of his men for one of mine fallen—
　　On, my bold heroes, and slaughter them down.
What though the wounded are dying around you,
　　Dead or alive like stars you will shine;
And if by good chance no bullet should wound you,
　　A fame that is matchless around you shall twine.
　　　　Then on to the field, ye brave sons of glory, &c.

See Alma's heights and Inkerman's valleys,
　　Balaclava, Odessa, where victory doth shine;
Onward! my armies, my true loyal allies—
　　Victory on victory till Sebastopol's thine.
O, shame on the man that would fly from the danger,
　　And lose the bright honour he'll win in the cause!
O! who would not die a courageous avenger,
　　In conquering the despots of Nicholas's laws?
　　　　Then on to the field, ye brave sons of glory,
　　　　　　On to the field where the balls round you fly;
　　　　Your names are enrolled in fame's golden story,
　　　　　　Your honour's immortal, and never can die.

The Lass o' the Glen.

WRITTEN AFTER READING A TALE OF THE BORDER.

I MET her when twilight was fast stealing awa',
When the sun's parting beams brocht the calm gloaming fa',
When the mavis was mute an' the fox in his den,
And I sighed and looked after the Lass o' the Glen.

Though dusky the e'ening, yet fu' weel could I see
There was life in her sweet smile an' love in her e'e,
And a worth in her bosom nae mortal could ken,
And my heart flew awa' wi' the Lass o' the Glen.

Syne I met her next day in the midst o' the chase,
So I pu'd up my reins an' I looked in her face,
And a thousand bricht guineas I vowed I wad spen'
That same nicht on a kiss frae the Lass o' the Glen.

Syne I met her again when the fox-hunt was o'er,
And she sat 'neath a tree by a wee cottage door,
So I tied up my horse tae its bark-buskit stem,
And I sat mysel' doon by the Lass o' the Glen.

But my memory was wove in a mystical spell—
I forgot a' my titles, my wealth, an' mysel',
And I wished frae my heart that kind Heaven wad sen'
But a blessing tae me wi' the Lass o' the Glen.

Syne I pressed her white han', and a kiss I did steal,
And I asked her a question I needna reveal;
But I thocht mysel' blessed aboon a' ither men
When I made Leddy Lyle o' the Lass o' the Glen.

Francis Best.

WRITTEN IN BELFAST, 1857.

Come all ye factory girls that work in Belfast town,
And if you want a song that's new, for you I'll write one down;
It is about a young man that's robbed me of my rest;
He is well known in Bedford Street—they call him Francis Best.

When I came o'er from Scotland's strand to Erin's shamrock shore,
There came with me a fine young man—my name he did adore;
And when he went away again my hand he kissed and pressed,
But the heart that fondly loved him then is gone with Francis Best.

He wrote to me three letters, and I no answer made,
And then he wrote to me a fourth, and in it this he said—
To know, dear Nell, who's won your heart, with grief I'm sore oppressed;
But little did young Willie know it was young Francis Best.

'Twas in a house in Sandy Row—that far-famed well known place—
That first I met young Francis with his comely smiling face;
The bright glance of his hazel eyes still beam upon my breast,
Both night and morn I see the form of my young Francis Best.

I cannot call him beautiful, nor can I call him fair,
Yet still there's something in his smile that makes him look so rare;
And always when I meet him he is so neatly dressed,
There's none I see so dear to me as my young Francis Best.

The factory men may laugh at me because I speak so plain,
The girls all in Sandy Row may look with cold disdain;
But let them laugh and let them look, my love I have confessed—
I feel no shame to own the name of my young Francis Best.

Now, all you factory girls, I have sung to you my song;
Although its music be not sweet, and all its verses long,
It is the language of a heart that hath the truth expressed—
When far from thee you'll think of me that loved young Francis Best.

The Lassies o' Dundee.

O WILL ye come to oor toon when the summer's blooming gay,
And see oor bonnie lassies, fair as the flowers o' May?
For beauty and for cleanliness, an' smiles o' winsome glee,
They bear the boast and wear the toast—the Lassies o' Dundee.

Tae see them in midsummer tripping gaily tae their wark,
The 'fair daughters of industry' cheerie as a lark,
Wi' rosy cheeks and witching een, like violets on the lea,
They'd mak' an auld heart young again—the Lassies o' Dundee.

When B—ks cam' ower frae England tae mak' a contract here,
And hire some o' the Saxon dames, sae orrie like and queer,
He spake lichtly o' oor lassies, being kilted tae the knee—
They paid him back wi' Scottish coin—the Lassies o' Dundee.

If e'er the Prince o' Wales comes back, and brings his bonnie bride,
We'll tak' them to the Baxter Park, whar beauty's queen resides,
And show tae them the princely gift Sir David did us gie,
For the health and recreation o' the Lassies o' Dundee.

Lang may oor merchants see their ships weel laden cross the Tay,
Whilst the summer sun is shining let our lassies gather hay,
For when the harvest it is gane the winter's ill tae dree—
A penny haned is tippence gained, braw Lassies o' Dundee.

May God send peace and plenty, and may want ne'er be oor doom,
And may oor garden o' commerce ne'er wither in its bloom,
And may oor bonnie lassies aye in virtuous honour be
The hope o' love and labour, and the glory o' Dundee.

O, gune ye'll come tae oor toon, ye'll see oor far-famed Tay,
That dines the river Clutha, the Fidoch, and the Spey;
Ye'll see oor bonnie factories like castles towering hie,
And ye'll get a sister's welcome frae the Lassies o' Dundee.

My Bonnie Donald Kay.

O! FAIR's the lily in the vale,
With slender stem and bosom pale,
And sweet's the summer evening gale
   When flowers are blooming gay;
And sweet's the rose upon the thorn
   When opening to the summer morn,
But sweeter far is thy fair form,
   My Bonnie Donald Kay.

Thy snowy brow, so mild and meek,
Thy ruby lips and rosy cheek,
Thine azure eyes whose glances seek
   To wile my heart away.
O! nature's beauty and her art
   Is centred in thy noble heart,
Thy every look a charm impart,
   My Bonnie Donald Kay.

O! were I Queen of Albion's Isle,
I'd give my crown to win thy smile;
Earth would seem heaven all the while
    When bound beneath thy sway.
To gaze on thy beauty is bliss,
And feel thy dear enchanting kiss
Clasped to thy bosom's kind caress,
    My bonnie Donald Kay.

Though thou art but a factory lad,
A royal princess might be glad
If she, like me, the pleasure had
    Of musing day by day.
It cheers my dark and lonely doom
When sadly bending o'er my loom,
To muse upon thy beauty's bloom,
    My bonnie Donald Kay.

Kennedy's Factory for Ever.[*]

OH, cheer, girls cheer, we have nothing to fear,
Glad nature lies smiling before us;
The sun shining bright, with his gorgeous light,
Is showering his love-beams o'er us.

---

[*] This song was sung by the authoress at the Giant's Causeway, on the memorable occasion of the annual pleasure excursion given by James Kennedy, Esq., to the workers in his Weaving Factory, Belfast, on Saturday, 31st July, 1858. The two ladies referred to in the last verse were from Manchester, on a visit to the Giant's Causeway. They were sitting at the well when the song was sung. They gave Miss Johnston a handsome sum of money to enjoy herself that day, saying at the same time, that they would never forget her singing 'Kennedy's Factory for ever.'

A day like this day again we ne'er may
Meet with while crossing life's river;
Then let us enjoy, without care or alloy,
And sing Kennedy's Factory for ever.
   Then we'll enjoy, without care or alloy,
   And sing Kennedy's Factory for ever.

This morn we did meet all in Bedford Street,
Now we're seventy-five miles from home;
And a happier band in Erin's green land
I am sure never met than our own.
We've music and mirth, a beautiful earth,
A master whose match we'll find never;
Then let us sing till the Causeway ring,
And sing Kennedy's Factory for ever.
   Then let us sing, &c.

Here's a toast to our master—the boast
Of all master's in green Erin's isle;
May he still have wealth; may we still have health
To remain his servants of toil.
His workers are we from all slavery free,
Oppressions vile chain we felt never;
His name we shall praise, our voice we shall raise,
And sing Kennedy's Factory for ever.
   His name we shall praise, &c.

We've all met this day at the Giant's Causeway,
Where Nature her works hath unfurled;
'Tis a gorgeous view; if history be true,
It cannot be matched in the world.
Those waters so bright, they gladden the sight,
That ne'er from our memories can sever;
The sea billows wave through yon echoing cave,
And sing Kennedy's Factory for ever.
   The sea billows wave, &c.

We sit round the well, and drink of its spell;
The poteen goes round by degrees;
Two ladies sit there, both handsome and fair—
Mrs Reison, her friend Mrs Lees.
From England they came to visit the scene;
Altho' from our land they must sever,
Wherever they be they will think upon me
Singing Kennedy's Factory for ever.
    Wherever they be they will think upon me
    Singing Kennedy's Factory for ever.

Linfield, the Boast of Green Erin.*

THOU star of our hearts, what rival can sever
That gold chain of glory that's linked round thy name;
Thou star of our hearts, what winter can wither
The laurels of honour that spring from thy fame.
Oh, thou art the gem of Murphy's brave men,
Fame's trumpet thy worth is declaring;

* This song was sung by the authoress in the Botanic Gardens, in honour of Mr Charles Close, manager of Murphy & Co.'s Spinning Mill, Linfield, Belfast, who gave the workers under his charge a pleasure excursion at his own expense, on Saturday, 10th September, 1858. That truth is stranger than fiction is beyond a doubt; and it has never been known, in history or romance, for a manager to do what Mr Close has done. He has shown a truly noble and sublime feeling of philanthropic love towards the humble sons and daughters of honest toil in Linfield; and it is the sincere request of the authoress that all those whose minds are so far enlightened as to be able to appreciate such a noble action, that they will cherish his memory with every mark of honour and respect. He has given a token of his heartfelt regard for the workers of Linfield, that shall be immortalised upon the pages of commercial fame and glory. He has also rewarded Miss Johnston most handsomely for her company on the memorable occasion.

O'er high hill and dale your praise doth prevail,
You've made Linfield the boast of green Erin.

Believe us, dear Close, you never shall lose
The good-will that all of us cherish;
This day what you've done, for you it hath won
A garland that never shall perish.
It's blossoms shall bloom, when o'er your still tomb
The sunbeams death's pale rose is rearing,
And centuries unseen o'er your memory dream
You've made Linfield the boast of green Erin.

Oh! where is the hand in Erin's green land
Would give us this day what you've given?
And where is the heart with gold thus would part, ?
You shall yet be rewarded by Heaven!
Our masters were kind, and we'll bear in mind
When unto Lord Lurgan's repairing,
We look'd not from you what you gave us so free,
You've made Linfield the boast of green Erin.

Long may you traverse its halls of commerce,
Our guide-star of commercial glory;
You've woven a chain that's emblazon'd your name
On the pages of fame's golden story.
Go when you will from Murphy's dear mill,
May peace be the lot you shall fare in;
To you we impart the prayer of our heart,
You've made Linfield the boast of green Erin.

Before you this day, where nature looks gay,
We pledge you how much you're respected;
Our heart's wish shall be, if on land or sea,
From all danger you'll still be protected.

May heaven above shower down her love,
A blessing for thee still preparing;
Our hearts' grateful theme shall still be for him
That made Linfield the boast of green Erin.

The Weekly News in the Morning.

Tune—'JOHNNY COPE.'

HA, ha! factory boy, are ye talking yet?
Is your hired bardie waking yet?
The press is on, and the types are set
    For the Weekly News in the morning.

We'll get something bright frae you;
But beware that a' ye tell is true,
For there's tae be a grand review
    O' the Weekly News in the morning.

The hale o' Scotland's men of lore
Will a' be roon the factory door,
And there shall be a sad uproar
    Wi' the Weekly News in the morning.

If ere anither lee ye'll tell
Upon their ain dear rhyming Nell,
They'll hing you up like a steeple bell,
    And wring oot yer tongue in the morning.

Ha! ha! factory boy, are ye shaking yet?
Is your 'Bardie's Reply' a making yet?
The printer's devil your doom has set
    In the Weekly News in the morning.

Rhyming Nelly.

FIRST VERSION.

Hark! the verdant blooming flowers,
Shooting from their vernal bowers,
Bawling in the diet hours—
    Ah! there goes rhyming Nelly.

Noo, every day that I pass bye
Wee Rhyming Nell tae me they cry;
Saul, but it mak's me prood an' high
    When titled Rhyming Nelly.

O, that's a name that I lo'e dear—
A name auld Scotland likes tae hear;
They canna gi'e me better cheer
    Than style me Rhyming Nelly.

Aye, that's a weel ken't honoured name,
That's lang enrolled in page o' fame;
I ne'er got cause tae blush wi' shame
    Since I was Rhyming Nelly.

Then, shout and bawl I dinna care
At dance, at market or at fair,
Or in the kirk at time o' prayer
    Sing out wee Rhyming Nelly.

An' gin ye see me on the street,
An' if a bonny lad ye meet,
O' send him wi a smile tae greet
    The far-famed Rhyming Nelly.

There's mony braw lads in Dundee
That fain wad hae a sicht o' me;
I'll stan a look although I be
    Wee withered Rhyming Nelly.

Then, shout and bawl wee Rhyming Nell,
An' waken a' the imps in ——,
Until the very deil himsel'
    Howls oot—Rhyming Nelly.

Rhyming Nelly.
SECOND VERSION.

THERE is a lass they ca' her Nell,
An' whiles she gets the Steam-Lim swell;
But whaur she lives I scarce need tell,
    For you're a' acquaint wi' Nelly.
        Nelly is a rhyming queen,
            Rhyming Nelly, rhyming Nelly;
        Nelly is a rhyming queen,
            Wha hasna heard o' Nelly?

When Nell did first gang tae the mill,
The weary shuttle there to fill,
Her tenter cried—Ye great numskull,
    O! that's only Rhyming Nelly.
        Nelly is a rhyming queen, &c.

Yae day there cam' a coach an' four,
Rattling to her mither's door;
The neebours a' did loudly roar—
    O! it's cam' for Rhyming Nelly.
        Nelly is a rhyming queen, &c.

Then oot there sprung a noble lord,
A marquis braw frae Oldenford;
They baith had sworn upon their sword
    They wad see wee Rhyming Nelly.
        Nelly is a rhyming queen, &c.

The morning licht did part the three,
For weel the jade could tak' a spree—
She was the soul o' mirth an' glee,
    And the lads a' liked Nelly.
        Nelly is a rhyming queen, &c.

She has rambled through the kingdoms three,
    And noo she's here in sweet Dundee;
In Glasca toon ere lang ye'll see
    The far-famed Rhyming Nelly.
        Nelly is a rhyming queen, &c.

Then drink to Nell a new-year toast,
For lang she's been auld Scotland's boast,
And may God speed the Penny Post
    That has made a queen o' Nelly.
        Nelly is a rhyming queen, &c.

Wanted, a Man.

MR EDITOR,
    I HAE a canty wee housie,
        I've got a' thing, frae pat to pan;
    And I'm a dainty wee lassie
        Jist wanting a coothie wee man.

Maybe ye winna believe me,
    But I live a fell irksome life;
Indeed I ne'er will deceive ye,
    I think I wad mak' a guid wife.

I'm guid at making and mending,
    And I can baith bake an' brew:
Some think me better at lending
    A han' for tae drink it, I trew.

I ken a lad they ca' Johnnie,
    I think, has a notion o' me;
He says I'm wonnerfu' bonnie,
    And blythe as a midsummer bee.

That my cheeks are like twa roses,
    That my e'en are a bonnie blue,
Like violets amang sweet posies,
    When kissed wi' the morning dew.

When I was just about twenty—
    Last June I was neat twenty-nine—
I could get braw wooers plenty,
    But few could I get to my mind.

Ilk ane had fauts but Jamie,
    But Jamie saw sad fauts in me;
When he won my puir heart frae me
    He then took a notion tae dee.

I vowed I'd ne'er coort anither,
    I'd ne'er be a living man's wife;
Noo I jist think it's a haver
    Tae live sae a eerisome life.

Gin I could get a bit manie
    Aye to welcome hame frae his wark,
And sing him a nice love sangie
    When I wad be clouting his sark.

I ken I could mak' him happy,
    If happy he wanted to be;
And whiles gie him a wee drappie
    Ilk noo and then in his tea.

Folk ca's me a wonnerfu' body,
    Jist as smart as a Pepper ghost;

A drap o' rum punch gars me study
    My muse for the famed Penny Post.

Noo gin ye will send me some chielie
    Ye think a fit marrow for me,
In your poet's corner I'll feel aye
    Most happy your servant tae be.

Song.

Why look on me as if thou loved me?
    Why fix on me thy bright blue eyes?
Whence came that magic power that's moved me,
    And thou perchance another's prize?
It matters not where'er I meet thee,
    Still through my soul their glances rove,
Thy winning smile comes forth to greet me,
    Borne on balmy wings of love.

Ah! if another's heart hath won thee,
    Yea, never gaze again on me,
But let thy smile for ever shun me,
    I cannot fan love's flame for thee.
But if a wife thou hast not chosen,
    Still smile on me where e'er we meet,
For I am one that loves to muse on
    Eyes that's bright and smiles that's sweet.

APPENDIX.

The Maid of Dundee to her Slumbering Muse.

Awake! my muse—ah! say how can'st thou slumber,
    Whilst feathered warblers chant their summer lays,
And Scotia's noble bards in countless number
    Are sweetly singing love songs in thy praise.

And weaving gems to deck thy crown of honour
    (Thou ne'er were worthy such a crown to win);
The God of Fortune seems to smile upon her
    Who sung thy lays amidst the factory din.

What recks it now how much the world may blame thee,
    Nor needst thou weep o'er cold contemptuous look;
Thy nation's heart in homage bows to claim thee,
    And thousands wait to read thy coming book,

Which thou composed when in the factory toiling,
    With aching heart and head beset with woes;
Which thou didst write, the midnight hour beguiling,
    When all the world was wrapt in sweet repose.

No marvel, then, thine eyes that once were sparkling,
    Bright as the costly diamond's radiant hue,
Have lost their lustre and are dim and darkling
    Amidst the tears which dyed their azure blue.

No marvel, then, thy cheeks that bloomed like roses,
　　Kissed with the dews which summer flowers inhale,
Are wan and withered, and a tinge discloses
　　Like sun-sick lily drooping in the vale.

For thine has been a task of love and labour,
　　Struggling for independence and for bread,
Through perseverance thou hast gained the favour
　　Of those that's showering blessings on thy head.

Fame's golden trumpet now is sounding o'er thee,
　　Thy praise it doth proclaim from shore to shore,
A world of hope and love lies spread before thee,
　　Thou wearst the crown no minstrel ever wore.

'Tis strange thy harp ne'er tuned a golden number,
　　Yea, half so rich as Tannahill or Burns;
Still thou art higher prized than those who slumber
　　Lamented much 'neath monumental urns.

Thy name and fame through every land is sounding,
　　Thy simple songs strange mystic charms unfurl;
And many a heart with hope and love is bounding,
　　To hail thy produce from thy Factory Girl.

But where are they who wrote those scandalous letters,
　　And sent them to thy lover o'er the sea?
Those false reports have burst the bridal fetters,
　　Though his faithful loving heart was bound to thee.

Weep not though they made thy lover doubt thee,
　　Though thou vowed his bride alone to be;
Go tell him now that he must live without thee,
　　Though once betrothed, thou now again are free—

Free as the wind that sweeps the stormy ocean—
  Free as the lark that soars the azure sky,
'Midst heavenly angels whispering their devotions
  When beckoning spirits to their home on high—

Go, tell thy swain to seek another lover,
  Whose name was never tinged with scandal in her life;
'Midst Queensland's bowers perchance he may discover
  Some other maiden meet to be his wife.

No man shall ever take thee to his bosom,
  Then gaze upon thee as a shattered wreck,
And cast thee from him like a withered blossom,
  Then say thou'rt only fit his heart to break.

'Tis better far that thou shouldst still live single
  Than married be, in doubts and fears to dwell;
When broken vows within the bosom mingle
  It only makes the home a demon's hell.

Go, tell thy foes that 'twas the wrongs they've done thee,
  That caused thy wailings in the Penny Post;
That crowned thee queen, and all those honours won thee,
  And made thee dear old Scotland's favourite boast.

Then go, my muse, and don thy robes of honour,
  Prepare to visit dear old Glasgow town,
Where thou shalt meet with many a noble donor
  Of those bright jewels that sparkle in thy crown.

Go, tell the Penny Post to wave its banner,
  And bid its minstrels sing that thou art free,
And they shall welcome forth in queen-like manner
  Thy Factory Girl—the maid of sweet Dundee.

Welcome and Appeal for the 'Maid of Dundee.'

Awake! my harp, that's hanging on the willow
    By Kelvin's river and the Three Tree Well,
Where hope sees sunbeams in the turbid billow,
    And builds a nest where nothing else may dwell.

Strike boldly, harp, for gifted Ellen, sounding
    Is all old Caledonia with her fame,
St Mungo's mighty men in wealth abounding,
    Think how she in your factories gained her name.

Ye who so lavishly are riches flinging
    On works of taste and monumental art,
To Gothic church, and hall, to all things bringing,
    (Save but the muse), gold with an open heart.

And fair young ladies, in the *boudoir* dreaming,
    Upon whose hands the time oft heavy falls,
When, by piano and guitar, is streaming
    The soft bright sunshine on the pictured walls.

Go, read in these warm days of shower and thunder
    The Factory Girl's latest July lay,
A piece that well may make the world all wonder
    Could *we* write like it? Tell me if ye may.

We, with our weary years of 'Havet's Grammar,'
    With dates, astronomy, and dear knows what,
And *parsing*, where the thoughtless often stammer,
    'Mid mood and tense, and case, and this and that.

Forgive me, ladies, if in zeal o'erstraining,
    Moved by the magic of my sister's lay,
It seem as if I had no thought remaining
    For you who were the gems of youth's brief day.

The *boudoir* then had diadems, and straying,
    'Mid these is memory now, bright maids were ye,
The circling stars that went with me a Maying
    Round Mr F., a zodiac to be.

Maggie, I mark again thy wit so sparkling,
    And Anne, I hear thy homily of sense,
While Rachel moves the tragic muse all darkling,
    And love and truth on Agnes' page condense.

Come one, come all, and help me who am bringing
    Some gems to grace the Factory Girl's crown;
Hark to the muse in memory's vista singing,
    And wreath forgotten garlands of renown.

And, factory girls, be proud that one's arising
    From your ranks so skilled in mystic lore;
Let others take the colours and be surprising
    In *art* as ye have been in *dress* before.

Prudence and Piety, I know you're scanning
    With cautious eye the long, long-looked for book;
I'm scarce the one to be your answer planning,
    Poets *find* the *fair*, but questions seldom brook.

God gave the mountain with the pine trees waving
    Over the purple heath and golden gorse,
And hoary oaks a hundred tempests blowing,
    And torrents roaring on their rocky course.

God made the mind linking a chain of mystery,
  Heights where the soul, like sun-eyed eagle, nests;
Slopes soiled by what is human in life's history,
  And depths more dark where still His sunshine rests.

I, as a poet, am that sunshine finding,
  And do not take the mountain, sand by sand,
Nor ceaseless circling thought am I unwinding,
  But 'tares and wheat' leave in the angel's hand.

For 'tares and wheat' in every book are blending,
  But scan the 'Book of Books' with deeper eye,
Where Heaven, the eternal sunshine lending,
  Shows in all things the soul of good to lie.

Farewell, old harp, in wayward measure singing,
  Wafting dry thoughts on idle wings of space,
Hang on thy willow while that Ellen's bringing
  More airy music with sweet playful grace.

Welcome a hundred times, my sweetest charmer,
  Whose witching strains taught my rude harp to sing,
Enchantress sent to make life's winter warmer
  O'er youth—o'er age thy spell alike to fling.

EDITH.

Printed in the United States
137397LV00007B/134/A